# Linux® Server Security

## Hack and Defend

## Chris Binnie

**Linux® Server Security: Hack and Defend**

Published by
John Wiley & Sons, Inc.
10475 Crosspoint Boulevard
Indianapolis, IN 46256
www.wiley.com

Copyright © 2016 by John Wiley & Sons, Inc., Indianapolis, Indiana

Published simultaneously in Canada

ISBN: 978-1-119-27765-1
ISBN: 978-1-119-27767-5 (ebk)
ISBN: 978-1-119-27764-4 (ebk)

Manufactured in the United States of America

10 9 8 7 6 5 4 3 2 1

For general information on our other products and services please contact our Customer Care Department within the United States at (877) 762-2974, outside the United States at (317) 572-3993 or fax (317) 572-4002.

Wiley publishes in a variety of print and electronic formats and by print-on-demand. Some material included with standard print versions of this book may not be included in e-books or in print-on-demand. If this book refers to media such as a CD or DVD that is not included in the version you purchased, you may download this material at http://booksupport.wiley.com. For more information about Wiley products, visit www.wiley.com.

**Library of Congress Control Number:** 2016937233

*I was terrible at school. I failed maths so many times, I can't even count.*

*—Stewart Francis*

## About the Author

**Chris Binnie** is a technical consultant who has worked online with Linux systems for almost two decades. During his career, he has deployed many servers in the cloud and on banking and government server estates. As well as building an autonomous system network in 2005 and serving HD video to 77 countries via a media streaming platform that he architected and built, he has written for *Linux Magazine* and *ADMIN Magazine* for a number of years. Outside of work, Chris enjoys the outdoors, watching Liverpool FC, and extolling the virtues of the unerring Ockham's razor.

## About the Technical Editor

**Rob Shimonski** (www.shimonski.com) is an experienced entrepreneur and an active participant in the business community. Rob is a best-selling author and editor with over 20 years' experience developing, producing, and distributing print media in the form of books, magazines, and periodicals. To date, Rob has successfully helped create over 100 books that are currently in circulation. Rob has worked for countless clients, including Wiley Publishing, Pearson Education, CompTIA, *Entrepreneur* magazine, Microsoft, McGraw-Hill Education, Cisco, and the National Security Agency. Rob is also an expert-level architect with deep technical experience in protocol capture and analysis, and the engineering of Windows and Unix systems.

# Credits

**Project Editor**
Adaobi Obi Tulton

**Technical Editor**
Rob Shimonski

**Production Editor**
Dassi Zeidel

**Copy Editor**
Marylouise Wiack

**Production Manager**
Katie Wisor

**Manager of Content Development and Assembly**
Mary Beth Wakefield

**Marketing Managers**
Lorna Mein
Carrie Sherrill

**Professional Technology & Strategy Director**
Barry Pruett

**Business Manager**
Amy Knies

**Executive Editor**
Jim Minatel

**Project Coordinator, Cover**
Brent Savage

**Proofreader**
Kathy Pope, Word One New York

**Indexer**
Johnna VanHoose Dinse

**Cover Designer**
Wiley

**Cover Image**
© TCmake/Getty Images, Inc.

# Contents

# Contents

## Contents

# Preface

There's little question that the knowledge required to secure systems and networks in an effective manner needs to be continually kept up to date. However, not all technical professionals want to become full-fledged security professionals; instead, they prefer to focus on other areas, despite their role demanding many of the required skills.

It seems like every other day the news reports another sensational attack and makes those working in the field count themselves lucky that their clients weren't the target. As our reliance on responsive connectivity and well-written software grows, so do the rewards for successfully compromising an online service.

The intention of this book is to offer a broad overview of both system and network threats. Rather than focus on one specific facet of online security, my aim is to examine a number of diverse areas, providing you, the reader, with enough knowledge so that you may pursue, in greater detail, those that interest you. Each of the chapters in this book explores aspects of security that I have found interesting on my journey as an Internet user, which, somewhat worryingly, now spans almost two decades.

The diversity of the subjects within this book will hopefully help you to secure your online services and also provide you the opportunity to experiment with common tools that hackers use. This is intended to benefit everyone, helping technical professionals to gain a better understanding of how attackers will identify and then try to exploit the vulnerabilities of a system or network. Elements of the knowledge contained in this book can be wielded to devastate online services, steal data, and reveal encrypted passwords. With great power ...

# Introduction

Consider for a moment that even highly publicized online attacks might be simple to carry out. The steps involved in launching an attack on a system or network can range from highly complex to frighteningly simple. This can be the case if a system is left unsecured with some well-known buggy software.

The modus operandi of a less experienced attacker may simply be the automation of seemingly endless port scans, opening a connection and promptly closing it, or tirelessly searching for a banner that reveals the version number of the service listening behind the port. If any versions match those listed in their vulnerability database, then a fresh target is identified by the attacker. Up to this point in an attack, as it is an almost fully automated approach, you might even say that it's nothing more than computers attacking computers.

Conversely, sophisticated attackers use a wide variety of approaches to disrupt or gain access to a system or network. They are not only experienced and intelligent, but also innovative, patient, and cunning. They employ social engineering, build customized hardware, and practice sleight of hand. During an attack, they adapt their methodology as the defender reveals their cards, and the attack evolves, sometimes rapidly. Much of the attack's impact comes from being well prepared; the sheer number of attack vectors that might be tested during initial reconnaissance is high.

Securing online services is a little like pushing water uphill, and I take no pleasure in saying that however well secured a service or system is, there will always be a way to breach or disrupt it. As bold a statement as that may be, keep in mind that even if a system or network isn't vulnerable today, there's an exceptionally high chance that it will be at some point in the future.

Sadly, this means that, barring the destruction of the power source for a server or networked device, the very act of switching on *any* electronic device effectively represents an attack vector for someone to exploit. This is a reality that technical professionals have long faced. The resulting approach to online security is one of weighing up how valuable the successful exploit of your online systems and networks might be to attackers versus the budget you have available to secure your infrastructure. You might also try to reduce the value of a single prize, for example, by separating your mail servers from your web servers. If one cluster of machines is compromised, then hopefully the other cluster will not be susceptible if it's behind a different firewall and using an alternative operating system.

Putting night terrors aside, thankfully, very few highly sophisticated attackers actually exist, against which your defenses will fail to one degree or another (sometimes within a matter of minutes). However, as the Internet matures, there are an increasing number of proficient attackers who can wield the power of other compromised systems and services, causing serious headaches for unsuspecting victims.

Furthermore, the motives for attempting attacks are varied and sometimes unpredictable. They might include receiving kudos from the hacking community, one-upmanship on a victim, a training exercise for wannabe novices, or simply financial gain. And, considering the most common demographic involved, let's not forget thrill seekers.

If your service is prone to certain types of unwanted attention, such as your web application being continually peppered with probes looking for security holes, then common sense dictates that you focus primarily on getting your developers to fix your application's flaws. Conversely, if you are running an e-mail service, then you need to be absolutely sure that the software that you opted to roll out across all of the mail servers in your cluster is kept up to date, and patched frequently and promptly. By focusing on the most obvious weaknesses, it's possible to limit the attack surface that you are likely to present to medium-skilled attackers, and to reduce the chances of them gaining a foothold on the rest of your infrastructure. Once you're content that your primary attack vector is mostly secured, you can concentrate on plugging the less obvious security holes.

It may help to focus your thoughts about security with a few simple questions. First, what are you trying to protect? For example, is there sensitive, secret information hidden deep inside a database, fronted by multiple firewalls and bastion hosts, or are you protecting an online service that absolutely must stay available to its users around the clock, every day of the year? This question is important because it affects how you bolster your defenses and potentially changes the defensive choices that you will make. You might, for example, pay top dollar every month for a network-traffic-cleaning service to help protect you against Denial-of-Service attacks, as opposed to buying several expensive, high-end hardware firewalls to secure your assets.

Second, how would you contain a security breach? If one server or device on your network is breached, then will that automatically mean other hosts will suffer the same fate? If that's the case, then clearly your security policy has serious issues that need to be addressed.

Third, how will you recover from a security breach? You might also be concerned about what happens if an attacker has discovered how your redundancy works and at what stage your failover services will be activated. There may be little point in simply rebuilding a primary server or blindly restoring network service if you don't know how an attacker managed to breach the security in the first place. Are you able to quickly restore services using an alternative vendor's equipment or software? If so, then you might reduce the likelihood of the same attack penetrating your security again, allowing you to restore some, if not all, services while investigating how the attackers got in.

# How This Book Is Organized

The chapters contained within this book can be read in any order and are a collection of security topics that have interested the author on his journey as an Internet user over the years.

The topics vary from the theory of past, current, and future attacks, to the mitigation and defense from a variety of online attacks, all the way to empowering readers to perform malicious attacks themselves (in the hope they will learn how to defend against such attacks).

By separating the various topics into chapters, the subjects can be referenced and returned to in the future to allow the reader to recount the content in greater detail. The content of each chapters is as follows:

**Chapter 1: Invisibility Cloak:** If an attacker can't see your server and isn't aware of its existence, then there isn't any attack vector to exploit in the first place. We discuss and demonstrate how to continue using services in production but without the unwelcome attention of attackers.

**Chapter 2: Digitally Fingerprint Your Files:** There are a number ways of keeping an eye on the integrity of your server's filesystems to ensure attackers haven't gained access. In this chapter we look at both a manual method and an automated tool that checks for rootkits.

**Chapter 3: Twenty-First-Century Netcat:** Steeped in history, the modern-day version of Netcat, thanks to its multitude of advanced features, has become a hacker's tool of choice. Learn how to spot if such a tool is being used against your servers and additionally how to utilize its industry-leading functionality.

**Chapter 4: Denying Service:** Only a handful of the world's largest Internet infrastructure providers can withstand the devastating effects of a full-fledged, high-capacity Distributed Denial of Service attack. In this chapter we discuss the topic in detail and even comment on an entire country losing Internet connectivity for three weeks due to such an attack.

**Chapter 5: Nping:** Knowing which services a host is running is only half the battle. This extension of the powerful Nmap security tool allows you to check just that on any host and also craft custom packets with unique payloads.

**Chapter 6: Logging Reconnoiters:** Although certain probes executed against your server might seem harmless enough, there is little doubt that being aware of how they work helps you secure your server further. We examine several facets of an attacker reconnoitering your server's vulnerable points.

**Chapter 7: Nmap's Prodigious NSE:** Many users will have used Nmap for simple port scans, but few know that the security tool includes the ability to exploit remote machines too. We explore just some of the many possibilities starting with the plethora of scripts that Nmap ships with by default.

**Chapter 8: Malware Detection:** A sometimes entirely silent threat that has plagued Windows systems for years comes in the form of illegitimately installed software. The damage that can be done to a system by malware ranges from annoying pop-up windows to full-fledged online banking compromises. In this chapter we learn how to deploy a sophisticated, frequently updated anti-malware solution on Linux.

**Chapter 9: Password Cracking with Hashcat:** Technical professionals might be alarmed to discover that one password-cracking tool all but guarantees that it can crack a hashed password. This means that if access to your hashed password is gained illegitimately, then it's just a matter of time before an attacker can see your password in plain text. This chapter walks you through the process, step by step.

**Chapter 10: SQL Injection Attacks:** In one prominent survey, SQL injection attacks were listed as the most prevalent online attack. Despite the fact that this type of attack dates back to the late 1990s, even today a frighteningly large number of such attacks successfully exploit websites belonging to enterprises and key online services through poor programming practices. This chapter offers some useful historical information along with step-by-step instructions on how to identify and exploit vulnerable online services.

## Who Should Read This Book

This book was written for mid-level admins, software hackers, and other IT professionals. It is however, hopefully, written in such a way that anyone who is curious will be able to quickly discern which sections are suitable for those interested in security but don't necessarily have a strong understanding of the Linux command line. The aim is that some readers will go on to research a specific chapter's subject matter in greater detail to help bolster their knowledge on that subject further, while other areas will be of less interest to their needs and potentially used for referencing at a later date.

In other words there is no difference in the levels of experience required on a per-chapter basis, although those chapters that focus more heavily on the command line may require greater effort for a novice.

## Summary

Let's hope that by increasing your understanding of a hacker's tools and mind-set, and staying on top of the latest security developments, you are not subjected to an all-too-common realization these days: that you no longer have control of your own systems or networks, but somebody else does.

# Invisibility Cloak

I magine that you could hide a server from the Internet but still have access to your ISP's superior bandwidth. Without making any changes, you would be able to securely use it as a file repository, among many other things.

You'd also have full access to the command line so that you could start and stop or even install any services that you wanted to use. The choice would be yours, whether you ran those services briefly and then closed them down, or left them running and visible to the outside world for a period of time.

This is possible to achieve using a technique called port knocking. You can disguise your server by closing all network ports to the outside world, genuinely making it invisible. The single port that you might choose to open up at will, by using a prearranged "door-knock," could be for your SSH server or for some other service. In this chapter, you'll see how you can create an invisible server along with some options that you might want to consider.

## Background

By disguising the very existence of a server on the Internet, at best you can run a machine in private, and at worst, even if its existence is known, you will reduce the attack surface that an attacker can target by limiting the time ports are open and even partially visible.

### Probing Ports

Before beginning, let's take a closer look at network ports on a server, so you'll have a frame of reference. If you've ever used security tools such as Nmap, then you may be familiar with the initially confusing premise that some ports appear to be closed when in fact they are not. Nmap makes the distinction between whether a nonopen port has a service (a daemon) listening behind it or not.

Nmap refers to closed ports as those that don't have a daemon listening behind them but do appear to be open or at least potentially available. If Nmap refers to filtered ports, it means that a firewall of some kind is preventing access to the IP address that is scanning the system in question. This is partly to do with TCP RST packets, and there are also three other states that Nmap reports back on: unfiltered, open|filtered, and closed|filtered. If you want more information on how these states are different, go to https://nmap.org/book/man-port-scanning-basics.html.

## Confusing a Port Scanner

Now that you know how ports may present themselves to port scanners, let's look at how to obfuscate the response you give back in order to confuse sophisticated port scanning techniques. The most obvious tool of choice, thanks to its powerful feature set, would be the kernel-based firewall Netfilter, more commonly known as iptables.

Here's how it works. For TCP packets, you want to manipulate how you respond to port probes by using iptables to generate a REJECT request. For other protocols you want to simply DROP the packets. This way, you get closed, not filtered, responses from Nmap. Based on what I've gathered from most online opinions (and it seems that this argument is both contentious and changeable), a closed port is the best response that you can hope for. This is because you're not openly admitting to blocking any ports with a firewall, nor is the port simply open because a daemon is running behind it.

To explain a little further, under normal circumstances, an unreachable port would usually generate an ICMP Port Unreachable response. You don't want these errors to be generated, however, because that would mean a server was listening on that port in the first place and you would give your server's presence away. The tweaked REJECT response that you want to generate instead is applied as follows:—reject-with tcp-reset. This helps you to respond as if the port were unused and closed, and also not filtered.

You simply append this snippet to the end of each of your iptables rules:

```
-j REJECT—reject-with tcp-reset
```

By using this technique, you're simply making sure you're not giving away unnecessary information about your system.

Note that in the port knocking example that you're about to look at, you won't be using that iptables option. This is because you won't be running additional services to your SSH server. However, this background information will help you understand how an attacker might approach a machine's ports and how you can apply a—reject-with tcp-reset option to other services.

There is some debate about using iptables DROP versus REJECT responses in your rules. If you're interested, you'll find some insightful information on the subject at

www.chiark.greenend.org.uk/~peterb/network/drop-vs-reject.

# Installing knockd

Now that you are armed with some useful background information, I'll walk you through how to install a port knocker on your server. As we continue you might consider which services you may wish to run hidden from the Internet at large. There might be an occasion to run a web server or a mail server on an unusual port for a few hours, for example.

## Packages

Let's look at installing the package that will give your system port knocking functionality. Called knockd, this package is installed in different ways depending on your system.

On Debian derivatives you install the package as follows:

```
# apt-get install knockd
```

On Red Hat derivatives you install it as follows:

```
# yum install knockd
```

A main config file controls most of the config required for knockd. On a Debian Jessie server, this file resides at /etc/knockd.conf. Take a look at Listing 1.1, which shows my main config file, to see how knockd works.

**LISTING 1.1   The main config file. The port sequences and (importantly) -I INPUT have been altered from the defaults.**

```
[options]
        UseSyslog
[openSSH]
        sequence     = 6,1450,8156,22045,23501,24691
        seq_timeout = 5
        command     = /sbin/iptables -I INPUT -s %IP% -p tcp—dport 22 -j
    ACCEPT
        tcpflags     = syn

[closeSSH]
        sequence     = 3011,6145,7298
        seq_timeout = 5
        command     = /sbin/iptables -D INPUT -s %IP% -p tcp—dport 22 -j
    ACCEPT
        tcpflags     = syn
```

## Changing Default Settings

In Listing 1.1, you can see a section for setting up your options at the top. The other two sections are the actions that you want to perform when knockd opens up SSH access or when you shut down your port access. Both sections also include the default port knocking sequence to trigger those actions under the `sequence` option. After installing knockd, I immediately changed those ports from the defaults to avoid reducing the effectiveness of my server security. The defaults are ports 7000, 8000, and 9000 to open up SSH access and ports 9000, 8000, 7000 to close access. As you can see, I've added more ports to open up the access so someone will be less likely to stumble across their combination with an arbitrary port scan.

After changing any settings, you can simply restart knockd as follows on systemd-based operating systems:

```
# systemctl restart knockd.service
```

After installing knockd, if you want more background information on the package, then Debian Jessie has a brief README file that you can find at /usr/share/doc/knockd/README.

This helpful README file discusses how knockd works, among other things. It uses a library called `libpcap`, which is also used by several other packages such as `tcpdump`, `ngrep`, and `iftop` (which capture packets for inspection). Thanks to its clever design, knockd doesn't even need to bind to the ports, which it's covertly listening on, in order to monitor raw traffic.

## Altering Filesystem Locations

Events such as connections, disconnections, or errors are logged directly to your system's syslog, and may be written to the /var/log/messages or /var/log/syslog file. If you don't want this information to be buried among other system log activities, or go to the bother of parsing an unwieldy log file, then you can create your own custom log file. I prefer to do this so that debugging is much clearer, and I might use an automated tool or a custom shell script to e-mail logs to myself daily so that I can monitor suspicious events. Because I'm keeping all knockd logs in one place, the information is easier to parse for scripts and other tools.

```
[options]
        LogFile = /var/log/portknocking.log
```

Changing the logfile's location is a common solution, but you can also alter where the Process ID file is written when the knockd service is launched. You can change the location under the [options] section of the config file, as follows:

```
[options]
        PidFile = /var/tmp/run/file
```

# Some Config Options

Now that you've got a better understanding of how the main config file is set up, you can examine how to configure it for your needs. Among a number of other tasks, you will consider how the timeouts of certain options play a part in setting up your server.

## Starting the Service

Don't be alarmed if you see an error message saying that knockd is disabled. This is a precaution so that until you have finished setting it up, knockd won't introduce unwelcome changes to iptables.

On Debian Jessie the error message asks you to change the following parameter to 1 in the file /etc/default/knockd:

```
START_KNOCKD=1
```

Clearly, you should only do this after double-checking your configuration or making sure that your out-of-band access is working as expected.

## Changing the Default Network Interface

Once you have configured your preferred port sequence, you might want to tweak other parameters. In the config file (/etc/default/knockd), you have the opportunity to alter the KNOCKD_OPTS settings. The example within that file is commented out and means that you can alter the network interface that knockd is listening on, as follows:

```
KNOCKD_OPTS="-i eth1"
```

These options will be appended to the knockd service, and you will need to restart your service to make the changes live, as follows (on systemd machines):

```
# systemctl restart knockd
```

## Packet Types and Timing

In the /etc/knockd.conf file, you can alter a few settings to finely tune how clients can connect to you. Referring back to Listing 1.1, under the [openSSH] section, you will add more options as follows:

```
[openSSH]
        tcpflags = syn
```

```
seq_timeout = 10
cmd_timeout = 15
```

The tcpflags option means that you can expect a specific type of TCP packet to be sent for knockd to accept it. That's a TCP "SYN" in this case. The TCP flags that you can use are fin, syn, rst, psh, ack, and urg. If the specified type of TCP packet isn't received, then knockd will simply ignore those packets. Be aware that this isn't how knockd usually works. Normally an incorrect packet would stop the entire knocking sequence from working, which would mean that the client would have to start again in order to connect. You can separate multiple TCP packet types by using commas, and it appears that newer versions (from version 0.5 according to the changelog) of knockd can use exclamation marks to negate the packet type, such as !ack.

Back to the other options in the example. You may have noticed that seq_timeout is already present in Listing 1.1 by default. However, because you have increased the number of ports within your sequence setting, you have upped the seq_timeout value to 10 rather than 5. This is needed because on a slow connection, such as via your smartphone, timeouts may occur.

The final option in the example is cmd_timeout. This option applies to what happens after knockd has received a successful knock. The sequence of events is as follows. First, once the port knocking has been confirmed as valid, knockd will run the start_command (refer to Listing 1.1 if you need a reminder). If this setting is present, then after knockd has executed the start_command option, it will only wait for the time specified in cmd_timeout before running the stop_command action.

This is the preferred way to open up your SSH server for access, and then promptly close it down once your connection is established. You shouldn't have any problems continuing with your session, but new connections will need to run through the port-knocking sequence again in order to connect. Think of this action as closing the door behind you once you've entered. Your server will become invisible again, and only your associated traffic will be visible.

## Testing Your Install

Because you are dealing with the security of a server, you should run a few tests to see that knockd is working as expected. Ideally you will have access to another client machine to run some tests from. To be completely sure that knockd is opening and closing ports correctly, I like to test by connecting from a completely different IP address. If you don't have access to a connection with a different IP address, then you might be able to drop your Internet connection periodically so that your ISP will allocate you a new dynamic IP address to test from. Some broadband providers will do this after a reboot or your mobile provider might too in addition.

## Port Knocking Clients

You can use different clients to create a knocking sequence in order to initialize a connection and open up your SSH port. You can even manually use tools such as Nmap, netcat, or Telnet to manually probe the required ports in sequence. The documentation also mentions that you can use the hping, sendip, and packit packages if they are available. Let's look at an example of the `knock` command that comes with the knockd package.

If you used the `openSSH` section shown in Listing 1.1, then you would set up your simple `knock` command with the following syntax:

```
# knock [options] <host> <port[:proto]> <port[:proto]> <port[:proto]>
```

I have configured TCP ports in Listing 1.1, so you can run the `knock` command as follows:

```
# knock 11.11.11.11 6:tcp 1450:tcp 8156:tcp 22045:tcp 23501:tcp
24691:tcp
```

The target host has the IP address 11.11.11.11 in this example. If you want, you can also put a combination of UDP and TCP ports in Listing 1.1; your client-side knocking sequence might look like this:

```
# knock 11.11.11.11 6:tcp 1450:udp 8156:udp 22045:tcp 23501:udp
24691:tcp
```

One nice shortcut is that if you only want to use UDP ports, then you can simply add -u to the start of the command rather than specifying them explicitly. You can run a command for UDP ports like this:

```
# knock -u 11 22 33 44 55
```

Let's return to your server's config file to see how TCP and UDP can be interchanged within your valid knocking sequence. In order to mix protocols, you would simply alter the sequence line under the `openSSH` section as follows:

```
[openSSH]
        sequence = 6:tcp 1450:udp 8156:udp 22045:tcp 23501:udp
24691:tcp
```

# Making Your Server Invisible

Once you are confident that your installation is working as you'd like, you can lock your server down to hide it from attackers. An attacker may be aware of the IP address bound to your server or may somehow be able to view traffic sent and received from that IP address (for example, they might work for the ISP that the server was hosted with).

Otherwise, it should be invisible to Internet users. I would experiment with your firewall if this is not the case. To achieve Nmap's closed port status, however, the following approach works for me.

## Testing Your iptables

As mentioned earlier, I will use the trusted iptables. Ideally you should have physical access to the server before locking it down, in case you make a mistake. Failing that, you should have out-of-band access of some type, such as access via a virtual machine's console, a secondary network interface that you can log in through, or a dial-up modem attached to the machine. Be warned that unless you've tested your configuration on a development box first, there's a very high chance of making a mistake and causing problems. Even though I've used port knocking before, I still get caught out and lock myself out of a server occasionally.

With that warning in mind, let's begin by looking at your iptables commands. Be careful when integrating these rules with any rules you already have. It might be easier to overwrite your existing rules after backing them up. First, you need to make sure that your server can speak to itself over the localhost interface, as follows:

```
# iptables -A INPUT -s 127.0.0.0/8 -j ACCEPT
```

You must now ensure that any existing connections are acknowledged and responded to, as follows:

```
# iptables -A INPUT -m conntrack—ctstate ESTABLISHED,RELATED -j
ACCEPT
```

You're using `conntrack` to keep track of associated connections. Your connections can continue to operate once they have been initiated successfully. Now, assuming that you're only going to open up TCP port 22 for your SSH server and no other services, you can continue. As a reminder of how to do this, referring to Listing 1.1, add the following command to open up TCP port 22:

```
command = /sbin/iptables -I INPUT -s %IP% -p tcp—dport 22 -j ACCEPT
```

Pay attention to this line. If you left an "append" by using `-A INPUT` in the command, you would be locked out by iptables. It must be an `-I` for "insert" so that the rule is entered as the first rule and takes precedence over the others.

You might be wondering what the `%IP%` variable is. Port knocking is clever enough to substitute the connecting IP address in the `-s` field, in place of the `%IP%` value.

Now here's where you have to be careful. There's no going back if this doesn't work the way you'd expect, so make sure that you have tested the rules on a virtual machine or that you have out-of-band access to the server just in case. You block all inbound traffic to your server as follows:

```
# iptables -A INPUT -j DROP
```

If you run the following command to check your iptables rules, then you won't see any mention of TCP port 22 and your SSH port:

```
# iptables -nvL
```

You will, however, see such a rule (very briefly if you've set up a low value for the cmd_timeout setting) in iptables once you have successfully logged in.

If you are having problems at this stage, then keep reading for some ways to troubleshoot your configuration and increase your levels of logging. Otherwise, you should now have a server whose ports all report as nonexistent, thus making the server invisible, as shown in Figure 1.1.

**FIGURE 1.1**

Nmap seems to think there's no machine on that IP address.

```
Starting Nmap 6.47 ( http://nmap.org ) at 2015-11-26 17:33 GMT
Note: Host seems down. If it is really up, but blocking our ping probes, try -Pn
Nmap done: 1 IP address (0 hosts up) scanned in 3.18 seconds
```

## Saving iptables Rules

To ensure that your iptables rules survive a reboot, you should install a package called iptables-persistent on Debian derivatives, as follows:

```
# apt-get install iptables-persistent
```

You can then save your rules with a command like this one:

```
# /etc/init.d/iptables-persistent save
```

Or, you can revert to the saved config by running this command:

```
# /etc/init.d/iptables-persistent reload
```

On Red Hat derivatives (on presystemd machines), you can use this command:

```
# /sbin/service iptables save
```

And to restore rules, you run this command:

```
# /sbin/service iptables reload
```

For the above to work on systemd Red Hat derivatives, you could try installing this package first:

```
# yum install iptables-services
```

# Further Considerations

There are a few other aspects to port knocking that might be helpful to you. Let's have a look at them now.

## Smartphone Client

On my Android smartphone, my preferred SSH app is called JuiceSSH (https://juic-essh.com). It has a third-party plug-in that allows you to configure a knocking sequence as part of your SSH handshake. This means that there's no excuse for you not to employ port knocking, even when you're on the road and without a laptop.

## Troubleshooting

If you run the command `tail -f logfile.log` on your port knocking log file, you will see various stages being written to the log. This will include whether a valid port is knocked, and importantly, if it was knocked in the correct sequence or not.

A debugging option also gives you the opportunity to increase the levels of logging produced by knockd. If you carefully open the file /etc/init.d/knockd and look for the OPTIONS line, then you can add an uppercase D character (Shift+d) to any existing values on this line as follows:

```
OPTIONS="-d -D"
```

The additional logging should be switched off once you have diagnosed and solved your issue to prevent disk space from filling up unnecessarily. The -d simply means run knockd as a daemon in case you're wondering. This should remain as it is for normal operation.

Back to the client for a moment. You can also add verbosity to the output, which the "knock" client generates by adding a -v option. Tied in with the debugging option, this should give you helpful feedback from both the client and server sides of your connections.

## Security Considerations

When it comes to the public information associated with your server, a reminder that your ISP should not be publishing forward or reverse DNS information about the IP address that you are using for your server. Your IP address should appear to be unused and unallocated in order for it to be invisible.

Even on your public services such as HTTP, you need to remember to obfuscate the versions of the daemons that are in use. The common way to do this with the world's most popular web server, Apache, is to change the "ServerTokens" to "Prod" and set "ServerSignature" to "Off". These are hardly cutting-edge configuration changes, but might mean an automated attack ignores your server when a new zero-day exploit is discovered because your Apache version number wasn't in its attack database.

Another aspect to consider is discussed in the knockd documentation. It mentions that if you use -l or --lookup service launch options to resolve hostnames for your log entries, then it might be a security risk. There's a chance of some information being leaked to an attacker if you do. The attacker may be able to determine the first port of a sequence if it's possible to capture DNS traffic from your server.

## Ephemeral Sequences

What about using a different approach to knocking sequences? It's also possible to use port knocking with a predefined list of port sequences that expire after they are used just once. Referring back to Listing 1.1 and your main config file, you can add this option to your open and close sections to enable one-time sequences if you want:

```
[openSSH]
        One_Time_Sequences = /usr/local/etc/portknocking_codes
```

If you remove the sequence line in Listing 1.1 and replace it with this code, then knockd will take its sequences from the file specified in the path instead.

The way that knockd deals with one-time sequences is unusual. It reads in the next available sequence from that file and then comments out that line following a successful connection with a valid knock. It simply adds a hash or pound character to the start of the line that has the sequence present. The next connection triggers the same sequence.

The documentation states that you should leave space at the start of each line. Otherwise, when the # character is added to the start of the line, you might find it has been overwritten unintentionally, meaning that you're locked out.

Inside your sequences file, you can add one sequence per line. That file follows the same format as the sequences option within the main config file.

The documentation also points out that you can put comments in by preceding them with a # character but bad things will happen (such as being locked out of your server) if you edit the sequences file when knockd is already running.

Once you understand the basic features of knockd, it is an excellent addition to experiment with. During testing, you could enter telephone numbers that you are able to memorize or some other sequence of numbers so that you're not continually looking up an insecure list.

For example, you might consider rotating through five telephone numbers, split up into valid port numbers.

## Summary

In addition to making your server invisible, I've covered how your server appears to the Internet before launching an attack. In order to fully obfuscate your server using port knocking, you should think carefully about public information such as reverse DNS entry, which might give away an IP address as being in use. You might also consider using NAT to hide a server and dynamically change its IP address periodically, only letting administrators know which IP address is in use at a given time via a secret hostname, published covertly in DNS on an unusual Domain Name.

There are many other facets to protecting a server; still, I've hopefully covered enough ground to make you consider what information is leaked to the public and may potentially be used in future exploits, as well as hiding a server if you need to do so.

# Digitally Fingerprint Your Files

There are a number of good reasons to keep an eye on your server security. Few sysadmin types absorb the necessary security knowledge required to keep their infrastructure safe without enthusiasm and effort. If you're anything like me, there have been a few bumps along the way, such as when I had a server compromised around the turn of the millennium thanks to a nasty PHP bug, or when I was faced with and repelled two relatively significant DDoS attacks.

This chapter will cover another attack vector, rootkits, and a fantastic piece of software called Rootkit Hunter (you may know it as rkhunter). You will start off, however, by exploring how to monitor your filesystem's important files, such as its executables.

## Filesystem Integrity

Many years ago I used Tripwire (`http://sourceforge.net/projects/tripwire`). It's now referred to as Open Source Tripwire, thanks to the availability of other products. Tripwire ran periodically (overnight using cron) and used cryptographic hashing to monitor any file changes on your system.

By generating and recording the hashes of any files visible on the filesystem initially, during its first run, Tripwire was able to alert the administrator if any hashes didn't match those it had recorded on each subsequent run. If the file had been altered in any way the hash would be changed. It's a clever approach, despite being I/O resource intensive on older hardware, and has since given birth to great grandchildren. One example is the popular AIDE (Advanced Intrusion Detection Environment), which is described as "a file and directory integrity checker" at `http://aide.sourceforge.net`. I would certainly recommend trying AIDE or Tripwire on a development virtual machine if you get the chance. Be warned, however, that if you are lax with the initial configuration, then you will be bombarded with false positives.

This type of security often appears under the umbrella of host-based intrusion detection systems, or HIDS, and it was reportedly one of the first types of software-based security because mainframes had few externally risky interactions over networks.

If you don't want to run nightly filesystem checks or you aren't in a position to receive daily system reports, then that's not a problem. You can opt to go for an older approach where you only scan your filesystem once, after you have built your server, in order to collect information about what files are installed on the filesystem. I will explain why this is useful in a moment.

You might be surprised that a tool you've almost certainly used for another purpose can be easily used as a security assistant.

Step forward the md5sum command. When downloading Unix-type files in the past, you have probably been offered the option to check the integrity of your potential download by verifying the MD5sums for those files. For example, the MD5sums are usually present on the website that you get your Linux installation ISO file image from.

As you can see in Figure 2.1, this is what you're faced with when downloading Debian Jessie from this Dutch mirror: http://ftp.nl.debian.org/debian/dists/jessie/main/ installer-amd64/current/images/.

**FIGURE 2.1**

You can download Debian Jessie from the website and also check your MD5sums for security.

| Filename | Time | Size |
|---|---|---|
| MANIFEST | 00:05 29-08-15 | 1709 |
| MANIFEST.udebs | 00:23 07-06-15 | 46432 |
| MD5SUMS | 00:23 07-06-15 | 53815 |
| SHA256SUMS | 00:23 07-06-15 | 72131 |
| udeb.list | 00:23 07-06-15 | 6337 |

If you open up the file MD5SUMS, then you can see the contents of Figure 2.1, which contains hashes for each file.

**LISTING 2.1    An abbreviated sample of the MD5SUMS file**

```
bf0228f479571bfa8758ac9afa1a067f   ./hd-media/boot.img.gz
ee6afac0f4b10764483cf8845cacdb1d   ./hd-media/gtk/initrd.gz
19fdf4efebb5c5144941b1826d1b3171   ./hd-media/gtk/vmlinuz
4dc2f49e4bb4fe7aee83553c2c77c9da   ./hd-media/initrd.gz
19fdf4efebb5c5144941b1826d1b3171   ./hd-media/vmlinuz
2750aec5f0d8d0655839dc81cc3e379f   ./netboot/debian-installer/amd64/boot-
    screens/adtxt.cfg
aca8674ab5a2176b51d36fa0286a40bb   ./netboot/debian-installer/amd64/boot-
    screens/exithelp.cfg
2e88361d47a14ead576ea1b13460e101   ./netboot/debian-installer/amd64/boot-
    screens/f1.txt
e62b25d4b5c3d05f0c44af3bda503646   ./netboot/debian-installer/amd64/boot-
    screens/f10.txt
```

Within Listing 2.1, in the left column, you can see the MD5sum of each file and the relevant filename to the right. This is to prevent someone else from sneaking a file into the place of a legitimate one, which could infect your clean operating system (OS) installation.

MD5sums first compute and then check against MD5 digests. You might think (in a relatively sophisticated way) that by checking MD5sums you are effectively creating a digital fingerprint for each file, which can be queried later.

You can easily try using MD5sums yourself (the MD5sum command is bundled within the package coreutils on my machine and should be readily available to almost all distributions). Try a command like this one:

```
# md5sum /home/chrisbinnie/debbie-and-ian.pdf
```

The response you receive might be something like this:

```
3f19f37d00f838c8ad16775293e73e76 debbie-and-ian.pdf
```

Now back to the files listed next to your Linux distribution. Download the MD5SUMS file into the same directory as the main ISO file (*ISO* is named after the ISO 9660 file system if you're wondering). By doing so, you can save yourself the trouble of manually checking each file on the installation media that you're using. This is because that file includes all MD5sums for the files in that directory. Now that you have the MD5sums for all the files, you can check them for validity with the following command (-c also stands for --check):

```
# md5sum -c MD5SUMS
```

Listing 2.2 shows the results from running the -c option. You might say that MD5sums are binary: results are either OK or not OK.

**LISTING 2.2  A sample of the output from checking against my MD5SUMS file using the -c option**

```
compare.png: OK
config2.png: OK
config3.png: OK
config4.png: OK
works_1.tar: OK
package_inst.jpg: OK
```

What should you look out for if a file didn't match its original MD5sum? In Listing 2.3 you can see that an alarm bell is ringing (with a FAILED warning) and that you are also informed of a problem at the end of the results.

**LISTING 2.3   An MD5sum that does NOT match and shows as "FAILED"**

```
test.sh: FAILED
bootstrap_AWS.pp: OK
hiatus.png: OK
md5sum: WARNING: 1 of 111 computed checksums did NOT match
```

It should go without saying that, without making these checks when you're installing your OS from a downloaded ISO or from a magazine's DVD, you are gambling with the integrity of your files and therefore risking your system's integrity.

Now that you've been reminded of how you can check if there's been any tampering with your freshly downloaded files, let's look at how to use the powers of cryptographic hashes to help you tell if an installed system has been compromised.

# Whole Filesystem

Once you're happy with your OS installation and have run through the requisite postinstall fine-tuning, you should consider recording the MD5sums of your key system files. You do this in order to have a reliable record to compare against during a suspected compromise.

Of course, doing this with the md5sum command probably isn't going to be very easy without writing a shell script; this is because it's difficult to get full directory trees of files working with the md5sum command.

Fear not, though: someone clever has addressed this problem with an efficient piece of software called md5deep (http://md5deep.sourceforge.net). According to its website, in addition to the functionality you can expect from MD5sum, you can also enjoy the following features:

You can

- Ignore certain file types (which is very useful when you want to ignore temporary files and so on).
- If you're inspecting a massive number of files (which you would on a fresh OS installation), then md5deep offers a very helpful ETD (Estimated Time of Delivery)—in other words, how long a command will take to complete.
- You can run md5deep in recursive mode to effortlessly pick up the numerous hidden subdirectories on your filesystem, which would otherwise be arduous (if not impossible to do accurately) to record manually.
- With compatibility in mind, you also import different types of hashes (for example, from EnCase, the National Software Reference Library, ILook Investigator, and HashKeeper).

I'm sure you'll agree that's exactly what you're looking for. Having completed your new machine's build, you can simply install md5deep and run it across your entire filesystem (or at least parts of it). One serious caveat is to keep the resulting hash list somewhere else than on the server. This is for obvious reasons. If your server is compromised, then it's very easy for an attacker to overwrite your MD5sum list with new, illegitimate MD5sums and deceive you.

If for some reason you can't get hold of md5deep (because you're working in a closed environment, for example), then it would be worth running the md5sum command over directories containing key binaries, such as this (nonexhaustive) list:

> /bin, /sbin, /usr/bin, /usr/sbin, /etc

# Rootkits

Let's now move onto a different approach to file fingerprinting.

If you're interested in protecting your files against rootkits (which contain code that allows someone else to access or control one of your machines), then you should consider an excellent tool called RootKit Hunter (also called rkhunter; http://rkhunter.sourceforge.net).

At install time, the RootKit Hunter manual warns that if you're trying to run the software on a presumably compromised system and the following standard commands or utilities aren't present, then you probably won't be able to run it successfully: cat, sed, head, or tail.

I'm pointing this out for good reason: these commands might be corrupt or missing on a compromised machine. If you've installed RootKit Hunter to hunt down evil files and you discover that your system has been compromised, then you really need to rebuild your machine. Don't assume that the remedial work you do from that point onward will make your machine secure enough for ongoing use. It's simply not worth it due to the time you will spend repairing the machine again in the future.

In other words, use software to identify successful attacks for exactly that purpose: identification. Also, always assume that you're going to need to run through a full rebuild afterward. I know from experience that these insidious rootkits are like filesystem limpets. You might find (as I have in the past) that you spend more time chasing your tail attempting to clean the system than a rebuild would actually take.

Lectures aside, let's look at using Rootkit Hunter. Once you have installed this sophisticated software, using the following commands, you can continue easily without any problem.

On Debian derivatives:

```
# apt-get install rkhunter
```

On Red Hat derivatives:

```
# yum install rkhunter
```

Assuming that your installation didn't throw up any errors, you can run a few simple commands to get started. The following command populates the file properties database with data about the files on your machine:

```
# rkhunter—propupd
```

Next, in order to scan any new software being installed and to trigger after software updates have occurred, you should enable the APT_AUTOGEN option to yes in the file /etc/default/rkhunter. I have only verified this on Debian derivatives with Apt Package Manager; there might be a different option on Red Hat derivatives.

Having made that change, you're now ready to make your first run of RootKit Hunter, as follows:

```
# rkhunter—check
```

Note that there are subtle differences between versions or distributions, so try adding -c or --checkall if errors appear.

Periodically you can also update your rkhunter threat list with the following command (you could create a specific cron job if you like) to keep track of the latest threats:

```
# /usr/local/bin/rkhunter—update
```

Figure 2.2 shows an abbreviated output that is generated after running this command. The output details the initial checks that the software makes.

As you can see, Rootkit Hunter is paying attention to the key directories that contain executable files (/usr/sbin in this example). These are exactly the types of binary files (among many others) that become infected by a rootkit.

Think for a moment of the Greeks and the Trojan horse allegory. In addition to those rootkits that immediately infect binaries, a piece of code can remain dormant for any period of time until executed by a legitimate user or on a schedule. Following that, a system compromise takes place.

**FIGURE 2.2**

An abbreviated display of the output from running rkhunter--checkall

```
[ Rootkit Hunter version 1.4.2 ]

Checking system commands...

  Performing 'strings' command checks
    Checking 'strings' command                  [ OK ]

  Performing 'shared libraries' checks
    Checking for preloading variables            [ None found ]
    Checking for preloaded libraries             [ None found ]
    Checking LD_LIBRARY_PATH variable            [ Not found ]

  Performing file properties checks
    Checking for prerequisites                   [ OK ]
    /usr/sbin/adduser                            [ OK ]
    /usr/sbin/chroot                             [ OK ]
    /usr/sbin/cron                               [ OK ]
    /usr/sbin/groupadd                           [ OK ]
    /usr/sbin/groupdel                           [ OK ]
    /usr/sbin/groupmod                           [ OK ]
    /usr/sbin/grpck                              [ OK ]
    /usr/sbin/inetd                              [ OK ]
    /usr/sbin/nologin                            [ OK ]
    /usr/sbin/pwck                               [ OK ]
    /usr/sbin/rsyslogd                           [ OK ]
    /usr/sbin/sshd                               [ OK ]
    /usr/sbin/tcpd                               [ OK ]
    /usr/sbin/useradd                            [ OK ]
    /usr/sbin/userdel                            [ OK ]
```

# Configuration

To configure Rootkit Hunter, you can edit its long config file, which can be found at /etc/ rkhunter.conf.

To receive overnight reports on the integrity of your machine, you just need to edit two config parameters, one defining the e-mail address of the recipient and the latter of which is adjustable if the standard mail command won't work on your system by default.

Once inside the config file, look for these salient lines, uncomment them, and adjust them to your needs:

```
#MAIL-ON-WARNING=me@mydomain   root@mydomain
#MAIL_CMD=mail -s "[rkhunter] Warnings found for ${HOST_NAME}"
```

The first line, once uncommented, specifies where to send the reports (multiple addresses can be separated by a space). The second line deals with the mail command and the subject line for the e-mail reports sent to those addresses.

Simply re-run the software with rkhunter—check to test if these changes work correctly and check your e-mail inbox.

To inspect the cron job that helps schedule when these reports will be generated, you can look in the file /etc/cron.daily/rkhunter. By default, cron.daily will generally run between 0100 hours and 0500 hours each morning on many distributions.

If you want to change how the e-mails look, then you can search for the following lines in the cron.daily file:

```
if [ -s "$OUTFILE" -a -n "$REPORT_EMAIL" ]; then
        (
            echo "Subject: [rkhunter] $(hostname -f)—Daily report"
            echo "To: $REPORT_EMAIL"
```

As ever, it might be prudent to create a copy of this file before altering it.

Back to the results that I generated from running Rootkit Hunter. In Figure 2.3 you can see some of the rootkits that Rootkit Hunter searched for.

**FIGURE 2.3**

A partial list of some of the rootkits that Rootkit Hunter searches for

```
Checking for rootkits...

Performing check of known rootkit files and directories
    55808 Trojan - Variant A                         [ Not found ]
    ADM Worm                                          [ Not found ]
    AjaKit Rootkit                                    [ Not found ]
    Adore Rootkit                                     [ Not found ]
    aPa Kit                                           [ Not found ]
    Apache Worm                                       [ Not found ]
    Ambient (ark) Rootkit                             [ Not found ]
    Balaur Rootkit                                    [ Not found ]
    BeastKit Rootkit                                  [ Not found ]
    beX2 Rootkit                                      [ Not found ]
    BOBKit Rootkit                                    [ Not found ]
    cb Rootkit                                        [ Not found ]
    CiNIK Worm (Slapper.B variant)                    [ Not found ]
    Danny-Boy's Abuse Kit                             [ Not found ]
    Devil RootKit                                     [ Not found ]
    Dica-Kit Rootkit                                  [ Not found ]
    Dreams Rootkit                                    [ Not found ]
    Duarawkz Rootkit                                  [ Not found ]
    Enye LKM                                          [ Not found ]
    Flea Linux Rootkit                                [ Not found ]
```

As you can see in Figures 2.3 and 2.4, there are a number of facets that Rootkit Hunter looks for; the checks are very comprehensive.

**FIGURE 2.4**

Another example of a comprehensive Rootkit Hunter search

```
Performing additional rootkit checks
  Suckit Rookit additional checks                      [ OK ]
  Checking for possible rootkit files and directories  [ None found ]
  Checking for possible rootkit strings                [ None found ]

Performing malware checks
  Checking running processes for suspicious files      [ None found ]
  Checking for login backdoors                         [ None found ]
  Checking for suspicious directories                  [ None found ]
  Checking for sniffer log files                       [ None found ]
  Suspicious Shared Memory segments                    [ None found ]
Performing trojan specific checks
  Checking for enabled inetd services                  [ OK ]
  Checking for Apache backdoor                         [ Not found ]

Performing Linux specific checks
  Checking loaded kernel modules                       [ OK ]
  Checking kernel module names                         [ OK ]
```

# False Positives

If you receive any false positives, then you can whitelist them within the config file /etc/rkhunter.conf.

If the volume of false alarms is a problem, then you can do this by uncommenting a config line that matches an entire directory within that main config file like this:

    ALLOWHIDDENDIR=/dev/.initramfs

If Rootkit Hunter incorrectly suspects that one of your binaries has been replaced by a script, then you can remove the warning with this option:

    SCRIPTWHITELIST="/usr/sbin/lsof"

For individual files you can also use this config setting:

    ALLOWDEVFILE="/dev/.udev/rules.d/99-root.rules"

Keep in mind that any hidden files or directories (those with names beginning with a dot) are almost always suspicious to filesystem scanners. In Figure 2.5 you can see another part of the Rootkit Hunter scan results that refers to checking for any malicious hidden files.

It's clear that the comprehensive checks made by Rootkit Hunter are well considered. Along with the filesystem and the process table, it also checks for networking anomalies, as you can see in Figure 2.6.

**FIGURE 2.5**

Part of the Rootkit Hunter scan involves the /dev partition and hidden files and directories.

```
Performing filesystem checks
  Checking /dev for suspicious file types       [ None found ]
  Checking for hidden files and directories      [ None found ]
```

**FIGURE 2.6**

The trusty Rootkit Hunter also makes a number of network checks.

```
Checking the network...

  Performing checks on the network ports
    Checking for backdoor ports                  [ None found ]
    Checking for hidden ports                    [ None found ]

  Performing checks on the network interfaces
    Checking for promiscuous interfaces          [ None found ]

Checking the local host...

  Performing system boot checks
    Checking for local host name                 [ Found ]
    Checking for system startup files            [ Found ]
    Checking system startup files for malware    [ None found ]

  Performing group and account checks
    Checking for passwd file                     [ Found ]
    Checking for root equivalent (UID 0) accounts [ None found ]
    Checking for passwordless accounts           [ None found ]
    Checking for passwd file changes             [ None found ]
    Checking for group file changes              [ None found ]
    Checking root account shell history files    [ OK ]

  Performing system configuration file checks
    Checking for an SSH configuration file       [ Found ]
    Checking if SSH root access is allowed       [ Not allowed ]
    Checking if SSH protocol v1 is allowed       [ Not allowed ]
    Checking for a running system logging daemon [ Found ]
```

# Well Designed

The Rootkit Hunter developers describe it as a "host-based, passive, post-incident, path-based tool." If you're wondering, the "passive" reference means that you need to schedule the software or run it manually. The "path-based" description means it just deals with files and doesn't operate heuristically like a virus checker might.

There is a section at the bottom of the documentation included with rkhunter that I enjoyed reading. It's a well-written primer for anyone who is new to online security or any experienced users who just need a refresher.

It first notes that before an attack is attempted, there is always some form of reconnoitering, so you should pay close attention to your log files. I remember having a script that watched out for traceroutes and ICMP traffic on one of my servers.

Again, repeating my earlier point, the manual goes on to say that this tool isn't a substitute for increasing the security of your machine. Don't treat it as one, but instead as a tool that helps to identify issues.

Interestingly, the Rootkit Hunter documentation also points you to one of their competitors, the excellent chkrootkit tool, which is an older incarnation. The manual suggests that only using one tool within a class of tools is sometimes not enough to gain all the information you need. Therefore, for the sake of completeness, you should benefit from the overlap that running both chkrootkit and rkhunter offers. That's a good point that should apply across all security facets.

Finally, the manual discusses what to do if you discover a compromise and you don't have the required skills to deal with a successful exploit. Along with going to www.cert.org, you may want to go to www.linuxsecurity.com.br/info/IDS/intruder_detection_checklist.html, which offers a list of steps for how to react to an online attack.

You are told by those with experience of such attacks that you should consider which authorities you can report the exploit to, and submit a report as soon as possible—instead of waiting weeks or months—in case something can be done to prevent other compromises. As ever, common sense applies.

# Summary

You're now armed with the ability to digitally fingerprint the files on your filesystem. As a result, you can quickly compare former MD5sums to see if your files have been altered, and also run Rootkit Hunter, either every night or periodically. The nice thing about rootkit checkers is that they also offer peace of mind by having a scheduled scan point out a config mistake that you've made. You can then hopefully remedy the mistake before it causes you further security issues.

From what I have covered, there are two rules that you should keep in mind:

- Always keep your recorded MD5sums (or any other hashes) somewhere safe (encrypted and password protected) and far away from the server.
- Don't rely on rootkit tools to reduce your efforts postevent; just use them to identify the issue. From there, figure out how a compromise was possible before you set

about rebuilding your machine. There's no point in spending a lot of time rebuilding a machine only to have the same security hole exploited again later. You might be shocked to hear how often this occurs.

When running less critical services, with a little forethought, the securing of a machine connected to the Internet usually doesn't involve too much work. And that's even when, inevitably, some time-consuming overheads are introduced, such as when overnight reporting is added on changes to your system. By taking precautions initially with your machine builds, hackers on the Internet can be held at bay so that you can get on with your work in peace.

# Twenty-First-Century Netcat

O ne of the first Linux packages that caused me to marvel at its capabilities was the powerful
netcat (https://nmap.org/ncat). There have been a few versions over the years, each
with a subtly different feature set. If you haven't used it, then you're in for a treat. It's been
described as the only tool that a sysadmin will ever need, which may be a little optimistic, but
netcat is genuinely exceptional.

For a start, it's incredibly lightweight, and its filesystem footprint is miniscule. In addition, a version of netcat is included in many distributions by default. After you've explored some of its background, you'll look at how you can use it to your benefit.

## History

Over the years there have been a number of implementations of netcat. The original Unix/Linux
version was written in 1995, and in 1998 a Windows version appeared due to its popularity. I once
read that a poll conducted by the Nmap Project (https://nmap.org) discovered that after their
own security tool, Nmap, their users opted for netcat as their second tool of choice.

Netcat's functionality also helped boost its popularity in nefarious circles. It's therefore commonly
used in attack reconnaissance (and attacks themselves) in addition to well-intentioned white hat
activities. As a result, you may not find full-fledged (modern) versions of netcat on enterprise
infrastructure, due to security fears and its packages being blacklisted as a threat.

I'll try to succinctly explain some of netcat's parentage. Confusion is easy because the original netcat (whose binary executable is called nc) was revamped by the Nmap Project, which refers to it as
"Netcat for the 21st Century." The result of the revamp was a binary called ncat. The man page for
ncat dutifully acknowledges the original version with the following closing comment:

> The original Netcat was written by *Hobbit* hobbit@avian.org. While Ncat isn't built on
> any code from the "traditional" Netcat (or any other implementation), Ncat is most defi-
> nitely based on Netcat in spirit and functionality.

This version of netcat (ncat) bills itself (modestly) as being able to "[c]oncatenate and redirect
sockets," but that's a gross understatement of its feature set.

There's a version of ncat available in Red Hat Enterprise Linux (RHEL) 7, for example, and I suspect, along with the original netcat (nc), it has been available in other releases in various incarnations over the years. There's also an original netcat version (bundled by default with Debian
Jessie builds, and whose binary is also called nc), and it headlines its abilities as being the

"TCP/IP Swiss army knife." The following RHEL 7 web page points out a few of the differences between these two incarnations: https://access.redhat.com/documentation/en-US/Red_Hat_Enterprise_Linux/7/html/Migration_Planning_Guide/sect-Red_Hat_Enterprise_Linux-Migration_Planning_Guide-Networking.html#sect-Red_Hat_Enterprise_Linux-Migration_Planning_Guide-Networking-New_network_configuration_utility_ncat.

If you visit that web page, you'll see that a number of command line options have changed. Either they no longer apply or the newer ncat might have simply changed their meaning.

It's also worth noting that without access to root user privileges, your success between versions may vary, so don't get too frustrated if it takes a couple of attempts to get netcat working the way you'd like. Here's an excellent article that shows you what to do when your version of netcat doesn't support the ?e or ?c options to run a shell: https://pen-testing.sans.org/blog/2013/05/06/netcat-without-e-no-problem.

Back to the RHEL 7 web page that I mentioned earlier. It states, with some confidence, that the newer ncat does not include certain functionality that its parent, netcat, did include. It may be that these features simply weren't as useful on the modern Internet. The NMAP Project website includes the following statement:

> Ncat adds many capabilities not found in Hobbit's original nc, including SSL support, proxy connections, IPv6, and connection brokering. The original nc contained a simple port scanner, but we omitted that from Ncat because we have a preferred tool for that function.

They are, of course, referring to their famous nmap port scanning tool, which they suggest should accompany ncat. In my opinion, they are a formidable force when coupled together, and I would suggest exploring the massive feature set that Nmap includes.

Back to netcat. Now that you're suitably confused, I'll further confuse things by mentioning that there were also two versions of the original netcat (I mean nc and not ncat in this case). The truly original netcat was written by Avian Research programmers in 1995, and the last version was released as version 1.10 in 1996. A GNU version of netcat was then released (http://netcat.sourceforge.net), whose most recent version, 0.7.1, was released in January 2004. The two "nc" netcats are worth mentioning because you may have difficulty using the same command line options between the two different versions. I've fallen into this trap in the past, and it caused a lot of head scratching when the documentation didn't match what the software was doing.

The Nmap Project's own netcat page (http://sectools.org/tool/netcat) also reveals that there were even more derivatives, including socat (www.dest-unreach.org/socat), Cryptcat (http://cryptcat.sourceforge.net), pnetcat (http://stromberg.dnsalias.org/~strombrg/pnetcat.html), and sbd (you will find an unofficial information site at www.question-defense.com/2012/04/09/sbd-backtrack-5-maintaining-access-os-backdoors-sbd).

# Installation Packages

For clarity, Debian Linux and therefore Ubuntu Linux use the package names shown in Table 3.1. On Red Hat derivatives, you might try this package name for a version of nc:

```
# yum install netcat
```

And for the Nmap Project's ncat, you might try this package:

```
# yum install nmap-ncat
```

I suspect that installing a package and then making sure you are reading the correct main page for that package (in case two versions of netcat are installed on the same machine) will prove successful.

**TABLE 3.1   Debian and Ubuntu Package Names**

| Package Name | Description |
| --- | --- |
| netcat | A "dummy" package for compatibility, which can safely be removed |
| netcat-openbsd | The OpenBSD package version with support for IPv6, proxies, and Unix sockets |
| netcat-traditional | The original package by Hobbit, which lacks many features found in netcat-openbsd |
| netcat6 | A rewrite of the original netcat with IPv6 support and enhanced support for UDP |
| nmap | This is the package that you need if you want to use Nmap's ncat on Debian/Ubuntu. |

To avoid confusion, I will be focusing on ncat (and the ncat command) as opposed to netcat (and therefore the nc command). I'll refer to ncat and netcat interchangeably from now on — or, of course, just ncat if further clarity is needed.

## Getting Started

Let's see what the twenty-first century's equivalent of netcat (by that I mean ncat, of course) can do for you, starting with some basics. Netcat boldly states that it contains powerful features that can manipulate data (both the reading and writing of data) from a network via the command line. It's highly reliable and can work with both TCP and UDP (it will also work well with IPv6). It can do impressive things with SSL (Secure Sockets Layer) connections and can also work well with proxies — both the SOCKS4 and HTTP "CONNECT" varieties.

Judging by the excellent programming practices involved in making the Nmap security tool, the quality of the ncat programming will also be very high. The Nmap netcat documentation makes a point of stating that it not only uses completely rewritten code (and doesn't borrow from the original version), but that it also employs Nmap's thoroughly battle-tested networking libraries.

Having mentioned HTTP proxies, I'll start by using netcat as a web browser. If you type this command, along with an arbitrary website you want to visit, then you'll be able to connect to TCP port 80:

```
# ncat -C www.chrisbinnie.tld 80
```

As soon as you've typed this command and hit the Enter key, you need to type the following text, and then hit Enter a couple of times:

```
GET / HTTP/1.0
```

Be warned that if you're not really quick, the command will timeout and you'll have to try again. If you've ever queried HTML from the command line before, then you probably won't be surprised at the excess of information that scrolls up your screen after doing so. If you're interested, the -C option throws a Carriage Return and Line Feed (CRLF) into the mix to allow for compatibility with some network protocols.

You can also use netcat as a daemon that listens. There are numerous ways of breaking into servers, and one way of leaving access open for a return visit is by leaving netcat listening on an obscure port that a sysadmin might not be aware of.

You'll think about that in a moment, but focus on HTTP for now. The ncat documentation provides an excellent example of how to turn your simple netcat binary into a basic web server. First, you will create a simple file. You won't use the .html extension, however, because your file won't be plain HTML; instead, it'll be one half of an HTTP conversation. You'll call the file index.http with the content shown in Listing 3.1.

**LISTING 3.1   One half of an HTTP conversation, saved in the file index.http**

```
HTTP/1.0 200 OK

<HTML>
<BODY>
Nothing to see here, move along.
</BODY>
</HTML>
```

As Listing 3.1 shows, it's mostly HTML, but the top line acknowledges the visiting web client's request first. Next you make netcat listen for connections, and present your file if it's asked to do so by running this command:

```
# ncat -l 127.0.0.1 80 < index.http
```

By the way, if you've just thought about serving all sorts of other content using netcat, then you're correct. If you've ever manually typed an SMTP conversation in via the command line, then you probably won't be surprised to discover that the <CR><LF> option — the -C option, that is — works just as well with e-mail conversations.

# Transferring Files

Think for a moment about moving a file from one host to another just using netcat at either end. You don't need complex SFTP daemons or resource-demanding applications for this.

You'll call your two example machines Lionel and Luis, and you'll watch Lionel passing a file to Luis. On Luis, you will run this command:

```
Luis> # ncat -l 1234 > bootstrap.pp
```

You can see that the -l switch simply asks netcat to "listen" for inbound traffic. You're listening for traffic on TCP port 1234, and you're outputting the inbound data to a file called bootstrap.pp; this file is a puppet manifest that you don't want to copy and paste between hosts because it's long and complex. Now that Luis is expecting to be passed some data, this is what you enter on Lionel to send it:

```
Lionel> # ncat --send-only Luis 1234 < bootstrap.orig
```

Having run this command on Lionel, the netcat instance on Luis will automatically quit. Before Luis has quit, it will output the contents of the file bootstrap.orig on Lionel to the file bootstrap.pp on Luis — a simple, clever action. The only things that might trip you up are, first, the versions (just use ncat for simplicity) and second, the firewall. Open your firewall carefully if you have firewall issues.

The ncat documentation also shows you how to use the tar command for moving multiple files. Consider this example:

```
Luis> # ncat -l | tar xzv
Lionel> # tar czv <list of files> | ncat --send-only Luis
```

As you can see, you're sending data from Lionel to Luis again, this time piping through the tar command at both ends. My favorite example is using compression to speed up the transfer (you can easily move massive files too) and, of course, transfer less data. Look at this method using compression:

```
Luis> # ncat -l | bzip2 -d > massive.file.bz
Lionel> # cat massive.file.orig | bzip2 | ncat --send-only Luis
```

In this example, you're using the trusty bzip2 command for the compression and then duplicating massive.file.orig on Lionel to a file called massive.file.bz on Luis. Note that you're using the cat command to read massive.file.orig and to pipe it into bzip2; that is not a typing mistake.

## Chatting Example

Let's have some fun chatting with a user on another computer. You may have seen the wall command in the past, which broadcasts to all logged-in users. You can use netcat for two-way chatting. Pick a port on the recipient machine (Luis again) and politely ask netcat to listen, as follows:

```
Luis> # ncat -l 1234
```

Next, run the following command. Having run that command, anything you type on Lionel (hitting the Enter key afterward to send each line of chat content) will be mirrored on Lionel's console, and vice versa.

```
Lionel> # ncat Luis 1234
```

In the following snippet, you can see how a conversation looks from Lionel's perspective.

```
# ncat 127.0.0.1 1234
Want to hear my two rules for success?
Ok!
Rule #1: Never tell anyone everything that you know.
Ok, and...
Hello, are you there?
```

This example shows one of many unexpected features that are included with netcat. I'll leave that functionality for you to explore and continue to examine some of the other options that are available. Netcat almost suffers from an embarrassment of riches in relation to its feature set, and there are simply far too many to cover here.

# Chaining Commands Together

One of the nice features included with ncat (but not nc) is the ability to chain multiple instances into a single command. This makes ncat very versatile; you can simply pipe the output of one netcat command into another, Unix style. Let's look at an example from the netcat documentation. For the following task, I'll introduce the machine "Neymar" as your third host. Lionel is still your sender, and in this scenario Luis is the man in the middle. Take a moment to look at these commands:

```
Neymar> # ncat -l 1234 > my_new_big_file.txt
Luis> # ncat -l 1234 | ncat Neymar 1234
Lionel> # ncat --send-only Luis 1234 < lengthy_file.txt
```

As you can see, in reverse, Lionel is passing his lengthy file onto Luis before he then chains the two netcat commands together in order to forward the file onto Neymar. This triumvirate works well, especially if Luis can't talk directly to Neymar because of a firewall or routing.

However, the documentation does point out a problem with this scenario. The issue is that Neymar can't talk back to Lionel. As you'd expect from the powerful netcat, there's a workaround. When I look at this example, I immediately think of exploits deployed for nefarious gain. (I'm sure you'll see why in a moment.) Now look at the following set of commands:

```
Neymar> # ncat -l 1234 > newlog.log
Luis> # ncat -l 1234 --sh-exec "ncat Neymar 1234"
Lionel> # ncat --send-only Luis 1234 < logfile.log
```

To my mind, the scary addition in this example is the -sh-exec option, which executes a new shell command when Luis receives data. Imagine the damage that you can cause with such an option, being able to launch any shell command. In this example, when Luis receives a connection, he spawns a new netcat instance and handles both the inputs and outputs of Lionel and Neymar's communications. It's very sophisticated.

Here is a port-forwarding example from the documentation, dealing with HTTP again, where you execute a shell command to forward traffic:

```
# ncat -l localhost 80 --sh-exec "ncat www.chrisbinnie.tld 8100"
```

You simply forward data destined for TCP port 80 on your local machine to another host on TCP port 8100.

# Secure Communications

I mentioned SSL earlier and how netcat can even interact with encrypted traffic, even though it's a worrying possibility to consider. I'll start this section with an example of how netcat can encrypt its own traffic. You use the -C switch again (sometimes called connect mode):

```
# ncat -C --ssl ssl.chrisbinnie.tld 443
```

Here you're assuming that your trusted machine, ssl.chrisbinnie.tld, is running an SSL server on TCP port 443 and you can therefore connect to it. Surprisingly, even for SSL servers that use certificates for authentication, the mighty netcat can be very useful.

You simply point netcat at the location of your PEM certificate and private key files, using the --ssl-cert and --ssl-key options respectively within the command. You can point both options at the same file if you like.

One important factor when exchanging certificates, along with encrypting communications, is the act of confirming (via a third-party service's stamp of approval) that the SSL server's identity is valid. Netcat is able to service such a request by using this command:

```
# ncat -C --ssl-verify ssl.chrisbinnie.tld 443
```

According to the documentation, netcat is able to check against SSL certificates as follows:

> Verification is done using the ca-bundle.crt certificate bundle shipped with Ncat, plus whatever trusted certificates the operating system may provide. If you want to verify a connection to a server whose certificate isn't signed by one of the default certification authorities, use the --ssl-trustfile to name a file containing certificates you trust. The file must be in PEM format.

https://nmap.org/ncat/guide/ncat-ssl.html

The docs continue and offer the correct syntax for an SSL command as follows:

```
# ncat -C --ssl-verify --ssl-trustfile <custom-certs.pem> <server> 443
```

Now that you can confirm which machine you are connecting to, let's look at another SSL function that is available to netcat. It has many applications, as you'll see when you explore it further.

This function is referred to as having the ability to "unwrap" SSL. The documentation suggests that if you're trying to collect e-mail from an SSL-enabled mail server but you don't have SSL capabilities available in your mail client, then netcat can assist.

You begin by pointing the aforementioned mail client at your localhost, your local machine, or IP address 127.0.0.1. With netcat listening locally on TCP port 143 (the port commonly used for unencrypted IMAP communications), you can then forward your traffic to the encrypted port on your mail server, TCP port 993, as follows:

```
# ncat -l localhost 143 --sh-exec "ncat --ssl mail.chrisbinnie.tld 993"
```

You can use this method for any protocol that uses two hosts, but HTTP, for example, won't necessarily work well when multiple hosts are involved.

Netcat can even act as an SSL server. You need to supply a certificate that, in a reversal to the previous example, might be verified by visiting clients.

Without specifying a certificate file and a private key — and using the same options as before (--ssl-cert and --ssl-key) — netcat will automatically generate them for you. You can start netcat by using the -l option (or its --listen equivalent) as follows:

```
# ncat -v --listen –ssl
```

As you can see in Figure 3.1, the accommodating netcat generates a temporary key to make things easier for you to get started.

**FIGURE 3.1**

Netcat automatically generates a temporary SSL certificate.

```
Ncat: Version 5.51 ( http://nmap.org/ncat )
Ncat: Generating a temporary 1024-bit RSA key. Use --ssl-key and --ssl-cert to use a permanent one.
Ncat: SHA-1 fingerprint: 7185 7CB4 7159 3F90 A0FC 5B26 46CE 0FA1 18D2 1EF4
Ncat: Listening on 0.0.0.0:31337
```

# Executables

Along with dealing with encryption, you can also execute a command on the shell upon receiving a connection. Needless to say, you must always consider the potentially disastrous security implications of running the following commands. Don't try anything on production machines without being very sure of what is going on behind the scenes. In other words, test these commands on development boxes first and become familiar with the considerable damage that they can do.

The first (worrying) executable example you'll look at is the Bash shell itself. It's not difficult to launch, which is very concerning. I have already mentioned that breaking into a server and leaving an alternative way of accessing it later is possible with netcat. With ncat you don't even need to be root to open up a shell. Try it yourself.

On your listening machine (Luis), whose shell you will open up to the world, you run this command:

```
Luis> # ncat --exec "/bin/bash" -l 1234 --keep-open
```

And in your familiar connect-to style (from Lionel), you simply run this command:

```
Lionel> # ncat Luis 1234
```

The first time you connect to TCP port 1234, you might suspect that the Bash shell hasn't been spawned correctly. However, try typing any valid Bash command, such as requesting a directory listing:

```
# ls
```

You will see Luis's current directory, but on Lionel's console, which should concern you. Type commands very carefully, as you won't get all the usual Bash feedback that you're used to, and file deletion and command execution is easy.

The highly popular and powerful security tool called Metasploit takes this functionality one step further, making the backdoor persistent. Even if you don't install Metasploit and further your knowledge, it's well worth reading this web page about using netcat on a Windows machine: `https://www.offensive-security.com/metasploit-unleashed/persistent-netcat-backdoor/`. You can see from reading this web page that it's relatively easy to write changes to the Windows registry and the firewall rules by following the included instructions.

Whichever operating system you are using, multiple options are available with netcat. Be warned that during your testing, you can pass many environment variables and cause all sorts of problems if you're not careful.

# Access Control Lists

With netcat the features keep on coming. You can even add ACLs (Access Control Lists) to your netcat instances. On a listening netcat daemon, you might add ACLs such as those in the following examples. You'll expand on the Bash command you just looked at by dutifully locking down your port, using an example from the documentation, as shown here:

```
# ncat --exec "/bin/bash" --max-conns 3 --allow 192.168.0.0/24 -l
8081 --keep-open
```

You can see that you're only allowing the 254 hosts from the CIDR /24 IP address range `192.168.0.0`, and machines are only allowed to open up a maximum of three connections. The combination of these options adds very welcome versatility.

The opposite of that command might be, using IPv6, a `--deny` example like the following:

```
# ncat -l --deny 1222:cb88::3b
```

Here you are allowing all other machines access and only denying this one. This applies equally to IPv4 as you'd expect.

Alternately, the following method is much more efficient when enabling or disabling access for multiple hosts. You simply populate a file with your entries. Use both `--denyfile` and `--allowfile` options as follows:

```
# ncat -l --allowfile trusted-hosts.txt
```

# Miscellaneous Options

Incidentally, you can easily jump from the default TCP by using the `-u` or `--udp` switches. You'll see why that's useful in a moment.

Similarly, to start using SCTP (Stream Control Transmission Protocol), you can provide netcat with the `--sctp` option.

Another handy tip is that you can also add up to three instances of the letter v, with -vvv offering the most verbosity when your commands output results.

In the same way that you used netcat to speak SMTP commands earlier, the powerful netcat is also capable of speaking Telnet commands. As a result, if you ever find yourself without access to a Telnet client, then netcat can also help out. There are a few obvious benefits to using netcat instead of Telnet. For a start, netcat is quieter and won't output data unless it is sent by the machine that you've connected to. There are also a few reserved control characters, which means that certain binary data will break if you're using Telnet. Also, you may have noticed that Telnet quits on quiet (idle) connections and stops running, which could mean that you won't receive the entire session's data. The Telnet command also doesn't work well with UDP but, as you know, netcat certainly does.

# Summary

I have only covered a tiny fraction of netcat's potential in this chapter; there's simply too broad a scope to cover.

Hopefully you understand that it's critically important to know about some of this sophisticated tool's features, if for no other reason than to reveal more about how an attacker might deploy them against you.

The next time I need to move files around inside a LAN, I'll be certain to use netcat; it's too easy to rely on more cumbersome data transfer tools such as SFTP tools for such simple tasks. You should avoid using the Telnet command for debugging open ports and connections and always use netcat instead.

In my case, I'll also have to remember not to show certain colleagues how to do any of the above, as there's a good chance that they will cause horrible damage and leave gaping security holes open.

3

# Denying Service

T here is no denying that without certain critical services working, the Internet would grind to a halt. Many users would suffer from degraded performance while others might simply experience a complete outage. Along with the DNS (Domain Name System), the NTP (Network Time Protocol) is key to the successful operation of the Internet. In this chapter, I'll spend some time describing how attackers might try to prevent critical services from working correctly.

Unfortunately for those who are responsible for keeping the Internet working, it's possible to attack large sections of the Internet's DNS and NTP infrastructure using a variety of methods. For example, DDoS (Distributed Denial of Service) attacks of the past were primarily designed to take an online service down or at least disrupt its users in a highly frustrating manner, possibly in order to gain a competitive advantage or receive payment of a ransom. Current thinking is that such attacks are now used as smoke screens to disguise other malicious security exploits.

One report, published in 2014 by Kaspersky Lab, estimated that small- to medium-sized businesses would spend around US$52,000 dollars on a DDoS attack. That figure would rise to around US$444,000 for enterprises that experienced such attacks. When you factor in loss of reputation, customer ill will at having to use slow online services (if they were available at all), and payment transactions failing (which might require manual involvement to be resolved postevent), guarding against such infrastructure challenges is a worthwhile activity. Most worrying is that out of 3,900 organizations across 27 countries that took part in the survey the report was based on, "[m]ore than one-third (38%) of businesses which provide financial services or operate public-facing online services have experienced a DDoS attack from April 2013 – May 2014."

The methods used to cause the denial of access to critical online services come in many forms. Having seen an increase in reflection attacks (amplification attacks included) over the past couple of years, on both NTP and SNMP services, I'll describe some of the history behind them, what is involved, and how to mitigate their potentially disastrous effects.

## NTP Infrastructure

I have touched upon the fact that critical infrastructure services are common targets for attacks because they present a high-value prize to an attacker. As DNS and NTP protocols have evolved over the years, security has, of course, been factored into their design. Consider NTP for a moment.

As you'd expect, there are built-in security mechanisms to assist with the toughening of NTP as a service. For example, some top-level NTP stratum-1 servers adopt a "Closed Account" option, and these servers can't be used without prior consent. Conversely, as you'd expect, as long as you adhere to their usage policies, OpenAccess servers are readily available for polling. Those RestrictedAccess servers can sometimes be limited for access due to a maximum number of clients or a minimum poll interval and are occasionally only available to certain types of organizations, such as academic institutions.

Another NTP security component is that the client software is written in a way to adhere to the instructions that are generated by those servers that they request the time from. If a recipient NTP server prefers to, then it can simply block a request. In a similar way to certain routing and firewall techniques, those packets are discarded or black-holed without intervention. In other words, the recipient server of these unwanted packets doesn't take on extra system load and simply drops the traffic that it doesn't think it should serve a response to.

However, such a response isn't always helpful, and it's occasionally better to politely ask the client to cease and desist, rather than ignore the requests unilaterally. For this reason, there's a specific type of packet called the Kiss-o'-Death (KoD) packet. If a client is sent an unwelcome KoD packet, then it will remember that server with an access-denied marker and look elsewhere for its timekeeping updates, or at least desist for a predefined period of time within rate-limiting thresholds.

There are other good reasons to watch the overall security of NTP. In addition to the demands on IP addressing and the impact on bank balances from bandwidth usage, you also need to include the Internet's NTP infrastructure on the list of services that are about to be affected by the potentially explosive, exponential growth of the Internet of Things (IoT). By all accounts, billions of additional devices will soon need to be synchronized, so that your refrigerator can order some more milk before you run out, among other things.

# NTP Reflection Attacks

Around the start of 2014, a nasty NTP attack surfaced, overwhelming Internet Service Providers (ISPs) and forcing the Internet community to act swiftly and effectively in order to contain it. For a short while, at least among victims of the attack, it caused significant confusion. The frighteningly simple but innovative exploit affected almost all NTP implementations. This attack was referred to as a reflection attack, which by its very nature generates otherwise unwanted traffic and points that traffic at a victim. This usually causes the victim to suffer load or bandwidth capacity problems unless they are supported by significant underlying infrastructure. In the past, these attacks have been referred to as challenge-response attacks; however, in my opinion that description isn't very helpful because not all reflection attacks involve authentication, and challenge-response is most commonly associated with authentication mechanisms.

The 2014 NTP attack followed similar DNS reflection attacks that had been witnessed frequently in the past. When such a critical service is discovered to have a previously unseen exploitable attack vector, there's a scramble by technicians wanting to protect their infrastructure. Decisions that they are faced with include whether that single service needs to be immediately disabled in order to keep other services running in the meantime, prior to a patch or configuration fix being made available. After all, it is possible to manually set the time on computers or in many cases allow for a slight inaccuracy of the system clock. Many services will survive missing 24 hours of synchronized NTP updates before any unwelcome effects are experienced.

Within these types of attacks, there are two terms that appear frequently. The first is *reflection*, which cognates to mirror-like redirection of attack traffic. Here, many third-party services usually respond by sending traffic to a victim (the main target), not the attacker. This is achieved by forging or spoofing the attacker's IP addresses and thus fooling the third party about who originally requested the traffic.

*Amplification*, on the other hand, might best be illustrated as sending one packet of data as a question and receiving one hundred packets in return as an answer. In the case of a reflection attack, this refers to the unsuspecting victim receiving the payload, or a sizeable answer to a question that they didn't ask.

Think of three machines in a triangle. Machine A asks machine C a lot of questions on behalf of machine B. Machine C then sends all of the answers incorrectly to B. Machine B is overwhelmed by the volume of answers. Machine A is invisible to B, and B doesn't even know that A is involved in the attack. For those protecting their infrastructure, this makes for a challenging diagnosis.

Reportedly the amplification ratio of the DDoS traffic generated by a standard DNS reflection attack is roughly 70:1. In other words, if you have one gigabit of bandwidth available to you, then you can forward 70 gigabits. The aforementioned reflection ratios made possible by the NTP exploit were reportedly from 20:1 to 200:1. You simply needed to look up a freely available list of public NTP servers to create a frightening amount of NTP traffic to fuel your DDoS attack.

The NTP attack was, as is often the case, horrifyingly simple. It was based around a built-in function that allowed anyone to query the last few hundred servers to connect an NTP server. The function that was exploited was called monlist; you may also see it appear as MON_GETLIST. An attacker spoofs the IP address asking the question so that the NTP server being queried replies to the victim instead of the machine submitting the query. By repeating that command again and again, the victim soon becomes overwhelmed if thousands of servers are responding simultaneously. The "amplification" of this "reflection" attack, where the amount of data involved in the answers is so much larger than the original question, is what makes it so devastating. This is because only a relatively small number of originating servers that are used to make such queries can topple vast sections of infrastructure.

The essence of mitigating such an attack, on an IPv4 system (the first line showing -4) and an IPv6 system (the second line with -6), comprises the following lines within your NTP config file:

```
restrict -4 default nomodify nopeer noquery notrap
restrict -6 default nomodify nopeer noquery notrap
```

4

A very welcome NTP server template, among others, that you can use to help your public-facing server to avoid being part of these attacks is available at www.team-cymru .org/templates.html. If you visit that page and click the Secure NTP Template link, you're presented with a collection of templates for various platforms including Cisco iOS, Juniper Junos, and Unix.

Also included is a useful reminder of how to configure IPtables to help lock down NTP, as follows:

```
# iptables -A INPUT -s 0/0 -d 0/0 -p udp --source-port 123:123 -m
state --state ESTABLISHED -j ACCEPT
# iptables -A OUTPUT -s 0/0 -d 0/0 -p udp --destination-port 123:123
-m state --state NEW,ESTABLISHED -j ACCEPT
```

In addition, there's an interesting note about the potentially damaging implications if you panic and decide to prevent NTP traffic into your network by blocking it at the router level. You should only filter UDP port 123 for NTP traffic if you know exactly what you are doing because, otherwise, key services will inevitably fail.

# Attack Reporting

When that first NTP attack took place, cloud service provider, CloudFlare, announced the largest DDoS attack ever recorded of its kind. According to CloudFlare, the attack was a little short of 400 Gbps of traffic and alarmingly only 4,529 servers were required to generate that much bandwidth-saturating traffic across 1,298 different networks. In contrast, a widely publicized attack that hit Spamhaus (the antispam service provider) reportedly used 30,956 open DNS resolvers to generate a 300 Gbps DDoS. As you can see, that's a significant difference in impact on a per-machine basis.

Another protocol that is being used increasingly in DDoS attacks was created in 1988 by PSINet, which was then one of the world's largest ISPs (if not the largest) before eventually becoming subsumed by various mergers and acquisitions.

The Simple Network Management Protocol (SNMP) is present on the vast majority of networking devices, such as switches and routers. This useful protocol helps feed statistical information, such as bandwidth use, back to any software capable of receiving it. Most important, enabled by default, is an attack vector based on a community string named "public". Even if passwords are configured by default, they tend to be simple, such as "private". This means that even your broadband router poses a potential risk and could participate in a DDoS attack. Also consider SNMP-enabled devices belonging to enterprises or ISPs; there might be dozens of powerful switches and routers on a single network segment with access to high-capacity bandwidth. As an aside, even printers in offices commonly employ SNMP implementations along with workstations and IP video cameras.

Attackers have been witnessed experimenting with SNMP for sizeable reflection/amplification attacks. The alarming traffic ratios are reportedly as much as 1700:1. How accurate that estimate is remains to be seen, of course, and whether a degree of scaremongering is present.

In May 2014, Akamai's DDoS division reported that they had spotted 14 SNMP attacks. Just under half were in the U.S., and around 18 percent in China.

# Preventing SNMP Reflection

Following a quick check of your `/etc/services` file, you can see the following details for the default ports used by SNMP:

```
snmp            161/tcp                        # Simple Net Mgmt Proto
snmp            161/udp                        # Simple Net Mgmt Proto
snmptrap        162/tcp                        # SNMPTRAP
snmptrap        162/udp       snmp-trap        # Traps for SNMP
```

To prevent the reflection of SNMP traffic originating from your network, you can follow a deny-by-default practice, making sure that your perimeter firewalls don't let any of this traffic out of your LAN and onto the Internet. Of course, this also applies to traffic coming into your LAN. So often, however, default settings are left unchanged when equipment is set up in a hurry, upgraded, or configured by unskilled personnel, resulting in these preventative measures being missed. What is most worrying about such an attack is that, thanks to the sheer number of broadband routers around the planet, it can take a long time to manually patch some of them (although responsible ISPs can add helpful ingress and egress filters to their networks). Meanwhile, large sections of infrastructure can start to suffer from performance issues.

The SNMP attack as described by Akamai was attributed to a specifically crafted attack tool. The tool automated SNMP "GetBulk" requests and spoofed the IP address, in the same way as NTP and DNS reflection attacks, in order to make sure the victim's IP address received the barrages of responses sent in reply to the spurious requests. Thankfully, this particular attack only applies to an older version of SNMP, version 2. Version 3 offers greater security and doesn't open itself up to as much abuse by default.

Worryingly, the key design of this attack was to generate significant amounts of traffic by only a few requests and possibly even from a single machine. Criminals can disrupt large sections of online infrastructure without needing to invest time and resources (and sometimes money to meet the purchase price of a botnet).

4

# DNS Resolvers

Near the end of 2014, another interesting attack came to light. It's still somewhat debatable if this was actually intended to be a reflection attack, but I'll discuss it here to add to your knowledge on the subject. As part of their services, Google offers two prominent DNS resolvers with memorable IP addresses:

```
8.8.8.8
8.8.4.4
```

These resolvers allow recursive DNS lookups for any individual or device that doesn't have a full-fledged DNS server available. These DNS resolvers will respond with any lookups you request, either from their cache or via a fresh lookup if a suitable answer doesn't exist in their cache. OpenDNS offers similar services but openly discusses the benefits of filtering your DNS queries, for the purposes of alerting you, for example, if you attempt to visit a previously reported phishing site. Their IP addresses are also easy to remember, resilient, and reliable:

```
208.67.222.222
208.67.220.220
```

These (mostly) free services are widely adopted, probably because they offer the convenience of not having the overhead of running DNS servers locally. However, thanks to their memorable IP addresses and outstanding reliability, sadly as with many popular services, these well-meaning providers present another high-value target that is attractive to attackers.

Clearly there are very good reasons to pay close attention to where you use such services within your production infrastructure, thanks to your lack of control should they be compromised. The most obvious attack, in terms of DNS lookup, might be DNS cache poisoning where the querying machine is given a false answer and sent to an illegitimate IP address, which could potentially infect the requestor or attack it in some other way. One of the many DNS cache poisoning attacks are so-called Kaminsky-style attacks (http:// dankaminsky.com), which don't just poison individual DNS records but rather take control of the authority records for a domain name themselves. There's some well-written information about security researcher Dan Kaminsky's findings at http://unixwiz. net/techtips/iguide-kaminsky-dns-vuln.html.

Because of their impact, the significance of DNS attacks should not be underestimated. Google's DNS resolvers reportedly serve in the region of 150 billion queries every day.

The 2014 attack, which on the surface included Google's DNS resolver IP addresses in the last quarter of that year, was picked up by popular online security channels. For example, the Internet Storm Center (https://isc.sans.edu) offered advice on spotting attacks purporting to come from Google's DNS resolvers as they arrived on your network. With some simple packet sniffing, it's possible to monitor this type of attack and log its frequency.

Here, using the tcpdump sniffing tool, you're simply dumping any pertinent traffic that you spot into a file called /tmp/suspect_traffic. You're categorizing that traffic as anything arriving from the IP address 8.8.8.8 (which is just one of Google's DNS resolvers) and destined for port 161.

```
# tcpdump -s0 -w /tmp/suspect_traffic dst port 161 and src host
8.8.8.8
```

By capturing this traffic, you can monitor its volume and whether the DNS queries are likely to be legitimate. If unwelcome traffic is discovered, you might want to restrict how those devices that are affected communicate outside of your network by introducing firewall rules. Firewalling offers access to the outside world for the devices in question.

Discussions between white hats and other security professionals suggested that these attacks, apparently sourcing traffic from Google's IP addresses, were actually designed (using the IP addresses that were preconfigured as the devices' DNS servers) to exploit and defeat poorly configured devices with other nefarious intentions, rather than being used to reflect traffic elsewhere. In other words, attackers could potentially reconfigure these devices for their own nefarious uses rather than deny their service.

For further reading, consider a separate attack vector and an attempt to circumvent legitimate BGP announcements (the Border Gateway Protocol is the sophisticated routing protocol that knits the Internet's many networks together) for Google's DNS resolvers; you can read more about it at http://thehackernews.com/2014/03/google-public-dns-server-traffic.html.

# Complicity

There is a set of recommendations that look at limiting spoofed traffic that leaves your network. Unfortunately, experience tells us that, whether it's through incompetence or lack of resources, there will always be a percentage of network administrators who fail to realize the importance of following such guidelines or who simply aren't equipped to pay attention to them. Not forgetting, of course, the small percentage of those administrators who purposefully leave holes open for criminal activities.

An older document was written in the year 2000 to stimulate debate and assist those with an interest in keeping the Internet running. Called Best Current Practice 38 (BPC 38; https://tools.ietf.org/html/bcp38), this document offers welcome advice to network administrators. Among other organizations, it encourages enterprises and academic institutions to toughen up varying aspects of their networking infrastructure, on both their hosts and networking equipment, to prevent cascading effects around the Internet.

Specifically, it takes some time to discuss the importance of ingress filtering to protect external networks from your own network if it is used as an attack tool. Citing that, by employing simple preventative measures, the diagnosis and mitigation of an attack from a "valid" source is far more effective than guessing where the originating traffic comes from, as you saw in the earlier section, "NTP Reflection Attacks."

Varying levels of ingress filtering should achieve that goal in many circumstances. One of the observations presented is that by reducing the number and frequency of attacks on the Internet, ultimately more resources will be available when attacks do occur. As a result, responses will be more effective. Much of the content contributed to these seminal guidelines is attributed to the venerable NANOG (North American Network Operators' Group; https://www.nanog.org) who vociferously discuss networking issues in detail on a popular mailing list.

# Bringing a Nation to Its Knees

The threat of multiple, geographically diverse systems being aimed at a single system — such as a networked or autonomous system, regardless of how large it may be — and taking it offline has long been a concern for enterprises, ISPs, and even entire nations. DDoS attacks may even have existed since the mid-1980s.

It was widely reported in 2007 that the Baltic state of Estonia suffered repeated DDoS attacks that, coupled with street rioting, almost brought the government to its knees. Apparently the population objected to the removal of a famous war memorial by the Estonian parliament. Coupled with a high level of social unrest, this was the final tipping point. The steadily increasing levels of attack traffic from the DDoS were received in a sustained manner over a prolonged period of time. News agencies were frustrated about the lack of connectivity, as this meant that the rest of the world could not be kept up-to-date with events as they unfolded within the country.

The Estonian DDoS evolved, and at one point reportedly involved four million packets per second of attack traffic. This was partly aimed at, and according to some reports was ultimately successful in, taking the nation's largest bank off the Internet. According to national statistics, around 97 percent of the population banked online, which meant this was a critical failure in the country's banking systems. And if the impact wasn't damaging enough already, the lack of Internet connectivity meant that the main bank couldn't communicate with, or dispense cash from, automated teller machines (ATMs).

Worryingly, it has been said that the only arrest relating to this hugely destructive incident, which lasted around three weeks, resulted in a fine worth less than US$2,000. NATO's involvement in furthering the effectiveness of international responses to these attacks was bolstered, however, by the stark lessons learned in Estonia.

# Mapping Attacks

As the excellent book, *Firewalls and Internet Security: Repelling the Wily Hacker,* by William Cheswick, et al. succinctly states in the Introduction:

> The Internet is a large city, not a series of small towns. Anyone can use it, and use it nearly anonymously.

> The Internet is a bad neighborhood.

The validity of this quote can be confirmed by using Digital Attack Map, an online tool that provides an excellent global overview of DDoS attacks and that is updated hourly, at www.digitalattackmap.com.

This fully graphical Digital Attack Map tool is run by Arbor Networks and Google Ideas, which populate the tool with data from over 270 global ISPs. These ISPs have agreed to share data with Arbor Networks' global threat intelligence system, ATLAS. The data is also available via Arbor's ATLAS threat portal and is worth a closer look at www .arbornetworks.com/threats.

In addition, there's a useful gallery that highlights key historical attacks for reference, at www.digitalattackmap.com/gallery. You can interact by hovering your mouse over the attack flows and revealing the eye-watering gigabits per second of bandwidth that were abused during the attack. There are also approximate sources of the attacks (for example, if an attack was generated by a botnet, then it might be from dozens of different countries), the presumed intended victim, and the attack's duration. Of additional interest are the source and destination ports used during the attack; lo and behold, the NTP port, UDP port 123, was present in one of the first few attacks that I queried. Interestingly, though, ports 80 and 53, HTTP and DNS respectively, still seem to be the most popular DDoS services, judging by the available data.

Figure 4.1 shows a sample of attacks from the Digital Attack Map website, along with the types of attacks and their color-coding on the left side of the global map. This is merely the splash page of this highly functional site. You could spend hours drilling down into both current and historical information that the site presents in an easily digestible format.

4

**FIGURE 4.1**

The comprehensive Digital Attack Map website from Arbor Networks, and powered by Google Ideas

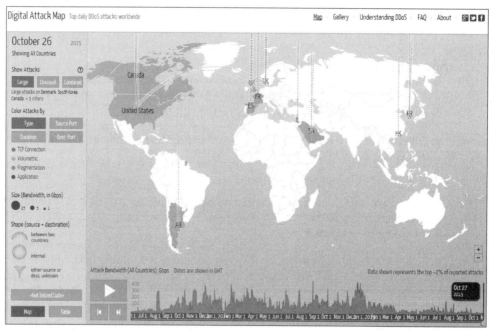

## Summary

In this chapter, we looked at a number of security issues that affect critical infrastructure services. These services, mostly affected using the more vulnerable UDP, genuinely help to bring the Internet together and clearly need to be protected. Some of these attacks are of an older design, but it is interesting to note how categories of attacks surge and diminish over different periods of time. For example, an attack that has not been seen for many years might resurface in a slightly more evolved state. As you saw more recently, the SNMP attack tools made available by the hacking community, most likely encouraged by the success of the NTP reflection attacks, have generated the most interest.

Even if it's not possible to follow the detailed intricacies of more sophisticated attacks, the premise is simple. Services relying on UDP are currently most at risk. UDP does not always expect a response (TCP enjoys a three-way handshake) and is therefore more likely to be exploited for reflection and amplification attacks.

You may previously have thought that following the initial lockdown of network services as they were being built (only partially opening up necessary services by using ACLs), these types of attacks would rarely impact a network or system's day-to-day operations. However, if you want your infrastructure to succeed in today's ever-changing attack landscape, it's imperative that you continuously monitor how your networks and systems interact with the outside world, revising ACLs and policies frequently.

That is an impossible feat to accomplish without diligently watching security lists and vigilantly following technical press announcements. Doing so, however, should mean that your Internet services don't become part of the problem and the global community can keep the Internet functioning.

4

# Nping

J ust as the U.S. military's DARPA (the Department of Defense's Defense Advanced Research
Projects Agency) contributed so greatly and helped to shape the Internet that you know and
love today, a similar military-to-civilian transition also resulted in the most common network-
discovery tool used on the Internet today: the ping command. The ping command's ancestry
stems from naval vessels sending sonar pings to detect if other vessels or geophysical features were
in the vicinity.

As part of the network discovery functionality that the powerful security tool Nmap (https://
nmap.org) provides, it also includes access to a powerful improvement to the standard ping command, called Nping (https://nmap.org/nping/). If you have used Nmap, then you'll know that
you're in safe hands with any tool created by the Nmap Project in terms of reliability and well-
considered functionality.

Let's look at how the Nping tool can help you gain more insight into what your systems and
networks are doing, digging into both remote and local connections.

## Functionality

On the surface, you might expect Nping's functionality to be relatively limited. After all, when you
fire off a ping, you send a question and then simply wait for an answer. Although Nping is still not
a finished piece of software, it's safe to say that it's a highly comprehensive and sophisticated networking tool.

You will begin by getting used to the syntax. You'll need to be logged in as root, the superuser, to
execute some Nping commands, and in this case, you'll look at TCP mode. Your first exercise will be
to fire off TCP "pings" (you read correctly; they're not ICMP pings) toward your local machine. From
the standard ping's man page, you can see that the normal operation of ping "uses the ICMP protocol's mandatory ECHO_REQUEST datagram to elicit an ICMP ECHO_RESPONSE from a host or gateway." In other words, there's a question and answer involved.

In case you're wondering, I'll be using my local machine for these examples to avoid upsetting any
other machines and populating firewall logs with suspicious activities. As with all white hat tools,
you should use them with great care.

Not only concerned with ICMP, the impressive Nping is a well-designed extension of the standard
ping command, which can also talk to many different protocols. It also gives you easy-to-under-
stand results.

If you don't have it installed already, you can install Nping as follows.

On Debian derivatives, simply use the following command to install the Nmap package:

```
# apt-get install nmap
```

On Red Hat derivatives, install Nmap using this command:

```
# yum install nmap
```

# TCP

Back to the TCP (Transmission Control Protocol) example. You'll run the following command against your local machine so that there will be no firewall issues to be concerned with and you won't upset other sysadmins:

```
# nping -c1 --tcp -p 80,443 localhost
```

Here you're sending one ping packet (with -c1 count option) over TCP, to TCP ports 80 and 443, to your local machine. The output from this command might look like Listing 5.1.

**LISTING 5.1   Having sent your first TCP pings with Nping, you are welcomed with a good level of detail.**

```
Starting Nping 0.5.51 ( http://nmap.org/nping ) at 2016-11-16 11:16 GMT
SENT (0.0145s) TCP 127.0.0.1:16463 > 127.0.0.1:80 S ttl=64 id=58041
    iplen=40  seq=2781160014 win=1480
RCVD (0.0148s) TCP 127.0.0.1:80 > 127.0.0.1:16463 SA ttl=64 id=0 iplen=44
    seq=2400211610 win=65495 <mss 65495>
SENT (1.0148s) TCP 127.0.0.1:16463 > 127.0.0.1:433 S ttl=64 id=58041
    iplen=40  seq=2781160014 win=1480
RCVD (1.0150s) TCP 127.0.0.1:433 > 127.0.0.1:16463 RA ttl=64 id=0
    iplen=40  seq=0 win=0
Max rtt: 0.079ms | Min rtt: 0.055ms | Avg rtt: 0.067ms
Raw packets sent: 2 (80B) | Rcvd: 2 (84B) | Lost: 0 (0.00%)
Tx time: 1.00054s | Tx bytes/s: 79.96 | Tx pkts/s: 2.00
Rx time: 2.00171s | Rx bytes/s: 41.96 | Rx pkts/s: 1.00
Nping done: 1 IP address pinged in 2.03 seconds
```

You can see in Listing 5.1 that you have received a reply from both TCP port 80 and TCP port 443. The pings stop themselves after each port has been sent data once (and data has been returned) as per the --c option. If there's no obviously valid response, then you might see something like this:

```
nping_event_handler(): READ-PCAP killed: Resource temporarily unavailable
nping_event_handler(): TIMER killed: Resource temporarily unavailable
```

Now that you have some idea of how Nping looks and reacts to your input, it should come as no surprise that you can use Classless Inter-Domain Routing (CIDR) network notation whenever you want (for example, 10.10.10.0/24). You'll stick with the basics for now and look at how to specify a range of ports to ping, rather than specifying them in a list as you've just done.

Consider the "privileged ports" on a Unix-type machine. These ports have been given a few names in the past (such as superuser ports or raw ports), but in essence, only the root user has permission to open them. This was an original security feature that meant if you remotely connected to one of these port numbers, you could be reasonably assured that the service running on it was genuine. In other words, it was spawned by the root user, not a standard user. Here is how to check all of the privileged TCP ports with Nping:

```
# nping -c1 --tcp -p 0-1024 localhost
```

Using a method that almost certainly differs from other networking tools, Nmap deals with multiple hosts and port numbers in an unusual way. For efficiency, if more than one target machine is specified, Nping won't simply send off a query to the first machine in the list and patiently wait for a response. Instead, it employs a simple but clever round-robin approach, where machines are contacted alternately in a rotation, so that no delay is introduced to the user when waiting for responses. With multiple hosts, this also applies with multiple ports to give the target a chance to recover before responding to the next port that Nping probes.

# Interpreter

Nping can act as an interpreter with a number of protocols. If you use the --tcp-connect option, then you are engaging Nping's TCP connect mode. Here you don't need to use root privileges to fire off what would otherwise be raw packets; instead, Nping asks the operating system to dutifully create the connections on your behalf. You can't see the contents of either inbound or outbound packets in this mode, but you can at least see the status of their transmissions.

As you would hope, the --tcp option, when run as the root user, enables you to achieve outstanding results with TCP packets. For example, you can attempt to manipulate the results of a connection by only partially completing a TCP handshake with TCP SYN messages. The documentation discusses the fact that there's a real possibility to do damage (actually, they use the word "evil") with customized TCP RST packets, spoofing IP addresses and closing down active TCP sessions, so be warned.

Here's how manipulating TCP handshakes might look if used as three separate commands:

```
# nping --tcp -p 80 --flags rst -c1 localhost
# nping --tcp -p 80 --flags syn -c1 localhost
# nping --tcp -p 80 --flags ack -c1 localhost
```

5

# UDP

You can also opt to employ the User Datagram Protocol (UDP) packets by using the --udp option. Normally TCP and UDP packets are embedded inside IP packets, but as I've said, without root permissions, as long as the default protocol headers haven't been changed, you can't see the content of the packets, just their transceiving status. The same applies to UDP packets.

A UDP ping can sometimes discover machines where other protocols fail. It's possible that a UDP ping might circumvent a firewall and report back if a device is listening behind that firewall. This is a very useful addition to your toolkit. A simple example command might look like this:

```
# nping --udp localhost
```

When I attempt to run this command against my local machine without being the root user, I see the following feedback:

```
SENT (0.0069s) UDP packet with 4 bytes to localhost:40125 (127.0.0.1:40125)
ERR: (0.0070s) READ to 127.0.0.1:40125 failed: Connection refused
```

However, as the superuser, root, I can complete the transaction as follows:

```
SENT (0.0161s) UDP 127.0.0.1:53 > 127.0.0.1:40125 ttl=64 id=64074 iplen=28
RCVD (0.0163s) ICMP 127.0.0.1 > 127.0.0.1 Port unreachable (type=3/
code=3) ttl=64 id=18756 iplen=56
```

As you can see, the UDP ping traffic is aimed at UDP port 40125 in both examples.

# ICMP

Just like the standard ping command, Nping defaults to using ICMP if executed as the root user when no other protocols are selected. The documentation boldly states that "[a]ny kind of ICMP message can be created." For example, you might query a time stamp, generate fake "destination unreachable" messages, or cause problems for another system or network by redirecting packets.

Try the following command logged in as both the root user and a standard user:

```
# nping localhost
```

You can clearly see the difference in detail. Here is the standard user, without much detail:

```
SENT (0.0027s) Starting TCP Handshake > localhost:80 (127.0.0.1:80)
RECV (0.0028s) Handshake with localhost:80 (127.0.0.1:80) completed
```

In the next example, as the root user, you can see that you are given more information about what was in the ICMP packet. The `type=8` entry stands for "8 Echo" according to its RFC (`https://tools.ietf.org/html/rfc792`), which is what you'd expect.

```
SENT (0.0152s) ICMP 127.0.0.1 > 127.0.0.1 Echo request (type=8/
code=0) ttl=64 id=31032 iplen=28
RCVD (0.0154s) ICMP 127.0.0.1 > 127.0.0.1 Echo reply (type=0/code=0)
ttl=64 id=18763 iplen=28
```

# ARP

You also have the `--arp` option, which allows you to experiment with the Address Resolution Protocol (ARP). In addition to deploying unwelcome ARP cache poisoning attacks, you can craft various types of ARP packets. The now obsolete RARP (Reverse ARP) lookups were used to translate a MAC address into an IP address. RARP has been succeeded by the BOOTP and DHCP protocols, but RARP still sometimes has its uses. There was also an evolved version of RARP called Dynamic RARP (DRARP), which is supported. It was mostly used by Sun Microsystems near the end of the last millennium, and is used very little these days. There's also support for "InARP" requests; this is similar to RARP but applies mainly to frame relay and ATM networks.

Finally, to complement these protocols, you can add `--traceroute` to the output to help determine which path traffic took by looking at the source address of "destination unreachable" packets sent in reply.

# Payload Options

Now that you're familiar with the main protocol options, let's see if you can take your new-found knowledge and put it to good use. Another reminder that Nmap was designed for white hat activities and should be used as such, not for illegitimate gain. It is possible to cause mayhem with tools of this nature.

If you wanted to add a payload to your probe packets, then there are three varieties, as shown in Table 5.1.

5

**TABLE 5.1  Payload Options and Their Descriptions**

| Option | Description |
| --- | --- |
| `--data` | Here you can append some hexadecimal data. The documentation offers examples such as `--data 0xdeadbeef` and `--data \xCA\xFE\x09`. |
| `--data-string` | You would append a string such as `--data-string "Per Ardua ad Astra"`. |
| `--data-length` | Using this option, you can fill a packet with random data from 0 to 65,400 bytes, such as `--data-length 999`. Be aware that anything over 1,400 bytes may overwhelm some network MTUs. |

# Echo Mode

Among the sophisticated features included with Nping is Echo mode. This mode is designed to show in detail what happens to packets as they traverse a network. By enabling Echo mode on two hosts, you can set up a server-and-client relationship to monitor exactly what takes place on the wire.

Let's have a look at this feature. The server component captures packets and then forwards details back to the client via a TCP communication "channel." It's the client's job to generate the aforementioned packets in the first place.

This technique is a great way to spot any packet-mangling should it occur. And, for example, if Network Address Translation (NAT) becomes involved, then a number of packet details are also changed. By using this technique if a device on the wire changes any other TCP options or if traffic shaping takes place, for example, then these otherwise difficult-to-diagnose details become apparent. You might also be able to determine where in transit packets become mysteriously blocked, which will assist in diagnosing issues.

Let's try a little experiment using Echo mode. Incidentally, you can add -vvv for verbosity if you want more output and a higher level of detail from Nping. To get started, you need to be the root user to spawn the server side of the connection. You will use the password "please_connect" and add verbosity to the output received on your eth0 network interface with the following command:

```
# nping -e eth0 -vvv --echo-server "please_connect"
```

The results of this command are as follows:

```
Starting Nping 0.5.51 ( http://nmap.org/nping ) at 2016-11-16 11:16 GMT
Packet capture will be performed using network interface eth0.
```

```
Waiting for connections...
Server bound to 0.0.0.0:9929
```

As you can see, your server is now listening for a client to connect on TCP port 9929.

Next, you'll generate some traffic by launching the client. Note, again, that here you're only using localhost, your local machine, for both the server and client elements of this test. Although it's not the best way of following traffic through a firewall or a NAT gateway, it should offer you enough information to understand how the process works.

You will also need to be the superuser to run this command. You will add the appropriate password and make sure that you connect to your localhost. Clearly you replace this option with the IP address of the remote machine you want to connect to, as follows:

```
# nping -vvv --echo-client "please_connect" localhost --tcp -p1001-
1003 --flags ack
```

As you can see, you're going to connect to three TCP ports (1001, 1002, and 1003) and then fire TCP ACK packets at them. If you have difficulties with the connection and you receive a "Handshake failed" error message, then you have probably entered your passwords incorrectly at one end.

Let's look at what happens on either side of the connection, starting with the client. As the root user, by adding the -vvv option, you're going to see inside the packets as they traverse the network; otherwise, the output would be much quieter. Listing 5.2 shows an abbreviated sample of what you see.

**LISTING 5.2  An abbreviated sample output from your client showing just one sent and one received packet rather than many packets**

```
Starting Nping 0.5.51 ( http://nmap.org/nping ) at 2016-11-16 11:16 GMT
SENT (0.4256s) TCP [127.0.0.1:20869 > 127.0.0.1:1000 A seq=33133644
    ack=4112791867 off=5 res=0 win=1480 csum=0x91F7 urp=0] IP [ver=4
    ihl=5 tos=0x00 iplen=40 id=4058 foff=0 ttl=64 proto=6 csum=0x6cf4]
0000   45 00 00 28 0f da 00 00   40 06 6c f4 7f 00 00 01   E..(....@.l.....
0010   7f 00 00 01 51 85 03 e8   01 f9 94 4c f5 24 39 3b   ....Q......L.$9;
0020   50 10 05 c8 91 f7 00 00                             P.......
RCVD (0.4258s) TCP [127.0.0.1:1000 > 127.0.0.1:20869 R seq=4112791867
    ack=0 off=5 res=0 win=0 csum=0x2E11 urp=0] IP [ver=4 ihl=5 tos=0x00
    iplen=40 id=0 flg=D foff=0 ttl=64 proto=6 csum=0x3cce]
0000   45 00 00 28 00 00 40 00   40 06 3c ce 7f 00 00 01   E..(..@.@.<.....
0010   7f 00 00 01 03 e8 51 85   f5 24 39 3b 00 00 00 00   ......Q..$9;....
0020   50 04 00 00 2e 11 00 00                             P.......
^C
Max rtt: 0.085ms | Min rtt: 0.083ms | Avg rtt: 0.083ms
Raw packets sent: 4 (160B) | Rcvd: 4 (160B) | Lost: 0 (0.00%)| Echoed: 0
    (0B)
```

*Continues*

**LISTING 5.2   An abbreviated sample output from your client showing just one sent and one received packet rather than many packets** *(continued)*

```
Tx time: 3.23067s | Tx bytes/s: 49.53 | Tx pkts/s: 1.24
Rx time: 3.23067s | Rx bytes/s: 49.53 | Rx pkts/s: 1.24
Nping done: 1 IP address pinged in 3.66 seconds
```

In Listing 5.2, you have abbreviated the output to only see one packet "SENT" outbound from the client to TCP port 1000. Next, the client receives a reply from the server (inbound, which is marked as "RCVD") from TCP port 1000 to TCP port 20869, one of the higher ephemeral ports.

The additional noise, thanks to the -vvv option, includes the checksum line (starting csum) and the three lines of content below. The ^C signifies that I've stopped the output just after it begins, for brevity. And, in the same way that the standard ping command behaves, you receive (rtt) Round Trip Times and transceiving statistics below, followed by an overall completion time.

On the server (also your local machine, which in reality is of little consequence), Nping is listening on TCP port 9929. Listing 5.3 shows the output that the server side produces.

**LISTING 5.3   The server's perspective of the packets that were sent by your client**

```
Starting Nping 0.5.51 ( http://nmap.org/nping ) at 2016-11-16 11:16 GMT
Packet capture will be performed using network interface eth0.
Waiting for connections...
Server bound to 0.0.0.0:9929
[1479294971] Connection received from 127.0.0.1:51099
[1479294971] Good packet specification received from client #0
    (Specs=8,IP=4,Proto=6,Cnt=5)
[1479294971] NEP handshake with client #0 (127.0.0.1:51099) was performed
    successfully
[1479294971] Client #0 (127.0.0.1:51099) disconnected
```

In Listing 5.3, your server has reported "Good packet specification received from client #0" and that a handshake was completed without any issue, followed by an Epoch time stamp of the disconnection from the client. There's not much more to glean from the server side, so you only need to be logged into the client if the server is always available for testing.

The Nmap Project helpfully provides some test machines that you can use. The password is "public" for the hostname "echo.nmap.org." For Nmap scans (not Nping), you can try this host: http://scanme.nmap.org.

Because NAT is so popular (and your connection is likely to be NATed), there's a good chance that you would see CAPT entries under the SENT lines and before the next RCVD line if you query that machine. This command works for me:

```
# nping --echo-client "public" echo.nmap.org --tcp
```

If you look carefully at the captured packet entries (CAPT), then you should be able to tell if NAT has altered your outbound source address. You would see a private IP address, such as 10.10.10.10, as per RFC 1918 (https://tools.ietf.org/html/rfc1918), being changed to show a publicly routed IP address such as 123.123.123.123 if NAT has been involved. It's relatively easy to detect NAT getting in the way of your connection. Remember that where there is NAT, there are sometimes also other devices altering MTUs (Maximum Transmission Units), packet-mangling for traffic shaping, unexpected firewalls, and invisible switches that might cause subtle changes to your connection.

There are a number of other scenarios within which Nping can assist, such as (after some learning) being able to spot if transparent proxies might be employed en route. I will leave you to advance your skills further, but in the meantime, the following section describes a few other options that you might find useful.

# Other Nping Options

Using the --delay 10 option, you can opt to limit the frequency of your packets. The default is to usually send pings at one second apart, but increasing this value can reduce the noise on your screen if you're watching diligently for a particular event.

Along the same lines is the --rate 3 option, where you can flood a target machine by sending three packets per second in the example just given. Don't get tripped up battling with the settings for the rate and delay options, however. According to the documentation:

> [t]his [rate] option and --delay are inverses; --rate 20 is the same as --delay 0.05. If both options are used, only the last one in the parameter list counts.

You can utilize the -H or --hide-sent option where outbound packets aren't shown. For example, if you're flooding a connection, then this will help.

In addition, if you're flooding a network and testing how it responds to a significant load, then you probably don't want to process each packet that is received. The -N or --no-capture option doesn't capture any packets that are received.

5

Many other command line options are available for Nping. For example, you can add `--debug` to assist you with more detail. You can alter TTLs (Time To Live settings). If you're scanning many hosts, you might also want to add a timeout option so that you're never asking Nping to wait around for a response with `--host-timeout 10`, where the 10 is a measure in seconds.

I briefly mentioned spoofing IP addresses in order to forge the sending IP address; Nping can go one step further and even populate the sender field with random values, by using a command like this to attack the host `whitehat.chrisbinnie.tld`:

```
# nping --arp --sender-ip random --ttl random whitehat.chrisbinnie.tld
```

Alarm bells rang when I first read about this feature. Being able to spoof an IP address with random values (successfully) should cause any sysadmin to be concerned. All it takes is poorly configured upstream routers to allow this type of traffic to arrive on an organization's network.

Finally, if you wanted to adjust the way the channel is used for Echo mode, then `--channel-tcp` or `--channel-udp` will do just that:

```
# ping  -vvv --client --channel-tcp 1234 --tcp -p 8100 localhost
```

As you might imagine, having the ability to adjust Echo mode to send its "channel" data back to the client via both TCP and UDP might be a lifesaver if a strict firewall gets in the way.

## Summary

If you experiment with Nping over time, you should come to appreciate that the reporting it offers is truly extensive. I'd encourage you to reach for Nmap whenever you have the opportunity, in order to gain more exposure.

With its packet-crafting possibilities, the powerful Nping can outdo many of its rivals. The addition of the sophisticated Echo mode means that if you have access to both ends of a connection, there's less chance of a device escaping detection. As a result, troubleshooting should be much swifter and less difficult.

Nmap's powerful Nping might be considered as just one tool inside a white hat's toolkit. By using tools such as these legally, you will excel at your intended tasks, and as a welcome afterthought, you'll learn how to keep your own servers up and running.

# Logging Reconnoiters

At times, you need to pay extra attention to who is connecting to your servers. For example, a series of attacks may have recently taken place, which you want to keep a close eye on, or you might just be super paranoid in general, thanks to the sensitivity of your data or the critical nature of your service.

One relatively unsophisticated approach to monitoring those machines that are making a reconnaissance of your servers would be to log the IP addresses that run pings and traceroutes against them. You may think that the information you manage to glean isn't going to be of much use, but it can actually be really important in building a picture of who connects to your servers, how often, and when. Akin to studying Closed Circuit Television (CCTV) video footage of people visiting an office, after a while, you get to know who stands out as unusual or who might not be expected on a given day. Log files are fantastic because you can forget about them only to return for analysis months later.

If you need to keep a vigilant eye on your servers, for whatever reason, then the trick to monitoring your system properly depends, in my opinion, on two things. First, you need a reliable daemon running in the background, listening like a sentry; it should be reliable so it doesn't introduce a race condition and cause your server to fail. Second, you need minimal logging so that you can go back to check your log file in a year's time and find the necessary information without worrying that the logs will overfill precious disk space and cause you further problems. Clearly you also don't want an attack to fill your disks with attack logs. That is unless of course you want to provision a high-capacity storage system and additionally are a fan of verbose logging.

In this chapter, you will explore how to log any nefarious reconnoiters of your machines and also how to counter potential Internet Control Message Protocol (ICMP) issues. You'll also learn how some attackers in the past took advantage of the good-natured protocol that is ICMP, and gain an overview of what common attacks looked like before ICMP gained a reputation for being insecure.

## ICMP Misconceptions

The traffic generated by pings and traceroutes uses the much-maligned ICMP, with UDP to a lesser extent for DNS lookups if required.

However, it's worth mentioning that ICMP was created for very good reasons and is still used for very important tasks in the day-to-day operation of the Internet. For example, it's needed to tell devices the size to set their Maximum Transmission Unit (MTU) in order to allow packets to traverse smoothly across heterogeneous network links. As a result, after reading what follows, you should avoid committing one of the most common junior sysadmin mistakes: blocking all ICMP traffic to your servers.

# tcpdump

Let's have a cursory look at your options for monitoring pings and traceroutes around the clock. Straight from the sysadmin's tool kit of reliable utilities, you might consider the powerful packet-sniffing tool, tcpdump. This tool has long been trusted to split traffic into smaller pieces in order to offer an insight into what is travelling across a network.

For example, if you want to pick up pings, then the following command works when I ping my paranoid server from another machine:

```
# /usr/sbin/tcpdump -i eth0 icmp and icmp[icmptype]=icmp-echo
```

This next example, showing tcpdump's ICMP packet-sniffing abilities, also picks up traceroutes:

```
# /usr/sbin/tcpdump ip proto \\icmp
```

As you can see in the following code, pings rely on both replies and requests; however, because my paranoid server's firewall is blocking certain ICMP traffic, an admin prohibited error is logged when traceroutes appear.

```
listening on eth0, link-type EN10MB (Ethernet), capture size 65535
bytes
17:06:47.925923 IP recce.chrisbinnie.tld > noid.chrisbinnie.tld: ICMP
echo request, id 21266, seq 1, length 64
17:06:47.925979 IP noid.chrisbinnie.tld > recce.chrisbinnie.tld: ICMP
echo reply, id 21266, seq 1, length 64
17:06:48.927871 IP recce.chrisbinnie.tld > noid.chrisbinnie.tld: ICMP
echo request, id 21266, seq 2, length 64
17:06:48.927921 IP noid.chrisbinnie.tld > recce.chrisbinnie.tld: ICMP
echo reply, id 21266, seq 2, length 64
17:06:49.928069 IP recce.chrisbinnie.tld > noid.chrisbinnie.tld: ICMP
echo request, id 21266, seq 3, length 64
17:06:49.928136 IP noid.chrisbinnie.tld > recce.chrisbinnie.tld: ICMP
echo reply, id 21266, seq 3, length 64
17:06:52.215139 IP noid.chrisbinnie.tld > recce.chrisbinnie.tld: ICMP
host noid.chrisbinnie.tld unreachable - admin prohibited, length 68
17:06:52.215179 IP noid.chrisbinnie.tld > recce.chrisbinnie.tld: ICMP
host noid.chrisbinnie.tld unreachable - admin prohibited, length 68
17:06:52.215194 IP noid.chrisbinnie.tld > recce.chrisbinnie.tld: ICMP
host noid.chrisbinnie.tld unreachable - admin prohibited, length 68
17:06:52.215210 IP noid.chrisbinnie.tld > recce.chrisbinnie.tld: ICMP
host noid.chrisbinnie.tld unreachable - admin prohibited, length 68
17:06:52.215220 IP noid.chrisbinnie.tld > recce.chrisbinnie.tld: ICMP
host noid.chrisbinnie.tld unreachable - admin prohibited, length 68
17:06:52.215231 IP noid.chrisbinnie.tld > recce.chrisbinnie.tld: ICMP
host noid.chrisbinnie.tld unreachable - admin prohibited, length 68
```

In the code snippet, a server called noid experiences probes from a host called recce. Recce is reconnoitering to see if the server is online.

# Iptables

You can also run the `iptables` command, which uses Netfilter's kernel-based firewall:

```
# iptables -I INPUT -p icmp --icmp-type 8 -m state --state
NEW,ESTABLISHED,RELATED -j LOG --log-level=1 --log-prefix "Pings
Logged "
```

If you're paying attention, you may have spotted the number 8 being used as the `--icmp-type` value. In Table 6.1, you can see the codes that are used by ICMP. You can find more information at its Request for Comments (RFC) page, at `https://tools.ietf.org/html/rfc792`. According to this page, ICMP has been around since 1981 or thereabouts, when the Internet was a very different animal.

**TABLE 6.1** **The ICMP Codes from the Kernel Source File, include/linux/icmp.h**

| Type | Code |
| --- | --- |
| 0 | Echo Reply |
| 3 | Destination Unreachable * |
| 4 | Source Quench * |
| 5 | Redirect |
| 8 | Echo Request |
| B | Time Exceeded * |
| C | Parameter Problem * |
| D | Time stamp Request |
| E | Time stamp Reply |
| F | Info Request |
| G | Info Reply |
| H | Address Mask Request |
| I | Address Mask Reply |

As a reaction to the attacks that used ICMP, changes were made to the Linux kernel over time. Thanks to the abuse of ICMP, the functions marked with an asterisk in Table 6.1 are rate limited by default in modern implementations of the kernel (since Linux 2.4.10).

In the following code snippet, you see the source and destination IP addresses (SRC=10.10.10.200 and DST=10.10.10.10) involved in the ping traffic exchange logged to the /var/log/messages file.

```
Feb 31 17:19:34 noid.chrisbinnie.tld kernel: Pings Logged IN=eth0
OUT= MAC=00:61:24:3e:1c:ef:00:30:16:3c:14:3b:02:10 SRC=10.10.10.200
DST=10.10.10.10 LEN=84 TOS=0x00 PREC=0x00 TTL=64 ID=0 DF PROTO=ICMP
TYPE=8 CODE=0 ID=40978 SEQ=1
Feb 31 17:19:35 noid.chrisbinnie.tld kernel: Pings Logged IN=eth0
OUT= MAC=00:61:24:3e:1c:ef:00:30:16:3c:14:3b:02:10 SRC=10.10.10.200
DST=10.10.10.10 LEN=84 TOS=0x00 PREC=0x00 TTL=64 ID=0 DF PROTO=ICMP
TYPE=8 CODE=0 ID=40978 SEQ=2
Feb 31 17:19:36 noid.chrisbinnie.tld kernel: Pings Logged IN=eth0
OUT= MAC=00:61:24:3e:1c:ef:00:30:16:3c:14:3b:02:10 SRC=10.10.10.200
DST=10.10.10.10 LEN=84 TOS=0x00 PREC=0x00 TTL=64 ID=0 DF PROTO=ICMP
TYPE=8 CODE=0 ID=40978 SEQ=3
```

If I used either tcpdump or iptables to log traffic, I would be keen to reduce the log files. The first reason for this would be to stop an attacker (knowingly or otherwise) from causing disk space problems by creating massive log files, after inundating a server with ICMP traffic. The second reason would be to keep the significant logging noise levels to a minimum so that I could quickly reference the log and spot what I was looking for.

Assuming that you wisely felt uncomfortable having tcpdump running in the background all year round, for reasons of system stability, let's use the iptables example to strip out the information that you need.

Let's look at a high-level overview of how you might go about stripping the noise out of a log. For clarity, you would probably want your reconnoiter logs to be dumped to a file separate from syslog.

I'm going to use the excellent, "rocket-fast" syslog server, rsyslog, as an example (you can find more information at www.rsyslog.com). This is because Red Hat and Debian (and their many derivatives) currently use rsyslog by default, so there's a good chance you will have access to it.

Let's take another look at the iptables pings example from a moment ago:

```
# iptables -I INPUT -p icmp --icmp-type 8 -m state --state
NEW,ESTABLISHED,RELATED -j LOG --log-level=1 --log-prefix "Pings
Logged "
```

You're now paying closer attention to the --log-prefix option, as shown here:

```
--log-prefix "Pings Logged "
```

If you want to save all kernel warnings to a new log file, then it is relatively easy to set up. Open the file `/etc/rsyslog.conf` and add the following line to the RULES section or close to it (assuming there's not already an entry for `kern.warning` that you might disrupt; otherwise, decide if you can overwrite or append to it):

```
kern.warning                            /var/log/iptables.log
```

Of course, when it comes to manipulating text files, you can achieve a lot of different results with a quick shell script (or by using some grep, awk, or sed command-line tools). However, for the sake of avoiding even temporary disk space issues, let's try not to log every warning from the kernel in case a piece of hardware starts misbehaving and logs thousands of warnings in a short period of time.

You're going to create a new syslog config file and call it `/etc/rsyslog.d/iptables-pings-logging.conf`. Incidentally, you can probably name this file whatever you like if your main config file (that's the `/etc/rsyslog.conf` file) picks up all config files that it finds in that directory. By default, there's an entry in that file that looks like this to read all the config files at once:

```
$IncludeConfig /etc/rsyslog.d/*.conf
```

I should say, however, that I had trouble getting the filters to work from a new file in that directory. That was despite checking permissions and having remote-syslog-logging working fine from within one of those files (and trying `startswith` and `regex` instead of the `contains` operator that you will see next).

If you run into the same trouble, then instead of adding the following two lines to your new config file, simply navigate to the line mentioning `kern.*` under RULES again in the main config file (`/etc/rsyslog.conf`) to avoid using a separate config file altogether, and add these two lines:

```
:msg, contains, "Pings"            /var/log/iptables-pings.log
& ~
```

The first line catches entries that include the string "Pings" and then asks syslog to write them to the file `/var/log/iptables-pings.log`. The second line is a little unusual and tells the syslog software to ignore any entries caught by the previous line so that you're not doubling up with your logs by writing the same content to another file. You can, of course, leave that second line out if you'd like to log elsewhere too.

Now that you're able to drop content to a log file and filter out specific iptables events (adding your own labels as you prefer), let's look at other examples.

# Multipart Rules

If you want to allow pings to reach your servers and also allow outbound pings from your server, then each operation involves slightly different iptables configuration.

The following web page explains how to allow pings into a certain IP address on your server (assuming you have more than one bound to your server) along with the different outbound pings config: www.cyberciti.biz/tips/linux-iptables-9-allow-icmp-ping.html.

Note that the -d for destination on the inbound ping rules means a specific IP address.

# Log Everything for Forensic Analysis

If you were concerned that you were experiencing an attack and you wanted to log all inbound connections to your machine, then you could (briefly) enable this command:

```
# iptables -I INPUT -m state --state NEW -j LOG --log-prefix "Logged
Traffic: "
```

Be warned that your /var/log/messages file would soon be very large, so you would have to disable the logging by flushing the rule as soon as you could. (You can check out the example later in this section to find out how to do this.) You might expect the output to look something like this from the iptables command:

```
Nov  11 01:11:01 ChrisLinuxHost kernel: New Connection: IN=eth0
OUT= MAC=ff:ff:ff:ff:ff:ff:00:41:23:4f:4d:1f:08:00 SRC=10.10.10.10
DST=10.10.10.255 LEN=78 TOS=0x00 PREC=0x00 TTL=128 ID=28621 PROTO=UDP
SPT=137 DPT=137 LEN=58
```

This extract is taken from my now sizeable /var/log/messages file. The traffic appears to have been generated by a Netbios packet. Simply swap INPUT with OUTPUT if you would prefer to track egested traffic.

On that note, what if you want to log traffic but also rate-limit what hits your server logs? Here's an example:

```
# iptables -I INPUT -p icmp -m limit --limit 5/min -j LOG --log-
prefix "Blocked ICMP Traffic: " --log-level 7
```

It's simple enough to change -p icmp to -p tcp or -p udp and pick up TCP and UDP packets, respectively. This example means that you are only logging five packets per minute of this type of traffic. This can be useful because, generally, the first few probes are informative before repetition starts.

Incidentally, if you find that your logs are filling up too quickly, then you can just flush every iptables rule like this:

```
# iptables -F
# iptables -X
# iptables -t nat -F
# iptables -t nat -X
# iptables -t mangle -F
# iptables -t mangle -X
# iptables -t raw -F
# iptables -t raw -X
# iptables -t security -F
# iptables -t security -X
# iptables -P INPUT ACCEPT
# iptables -P FORWARD ACCEPT
# iptables -P OUTPUT ACCEPT
```

My preference is to put this string of commands into a script (or very long Bash alias, with the commands separated by semicolons), and as the root user, I can type **flush** whenever I need a quick, fail-safe removal of all the firewall rules in use.

# Hardening

If you're worried about your system being overloaded with ICMP traffic, then there are a couple of relatively simple things you can check. This is thanks to the power of Unix-type operating systems. First (and your build may already have this set as default), you can ignore ICMP broadcasts by adding the following line to the bottom of the file /etc/sys-ctl.conf:

```
net.ipv4.icmp_echo_ignore_broadcasts = 1
```

This sysctl.conf example will persist a reboot, whereas the following command will set it live immediately:

```
# echo "1" > /proc/sys/net/ipv4/icmp_echo_ignore_broadcasts
```

The following command will also set it live immediately if you have followed the sysctl.conf example (it reloads all the config settings found inside the file sysctl.conf):

```
# sysctl -p
```

The icmp_echo_ignore_broadcasts setting stops ICMP broadcasts from bringing down your network with unwanted broadcast traffic.

In reality, this is a deprecated attack (you saw that modern kernels use rate-limiting as standard), and the kernel setting is really only useful for ping attacks to the broadcast address that force every device in the local network's broadcast domain to respond. If every device responds at the same time and then responds to others' responses, then a denial of service is caused by too much traffic on the network. As with all kernel settings, though, it's useful to know the background to help you understand how networking works.

Another attack (harking from 1996) was called the Ping of Death, and crafted massive ICMP packets with the hope of crashing the remote machine. It affected many of the popular networking stacks (at release 18 operating systems were found to be vulnerable). Simply knowing an IP address and firing ICMP packets greater than 65,536 bytes at that IP address caused the machine to which it was bound to crash. There's more information from the excellent Insecure.org website, at `http://insecure.org/sploits/ping-o-death.html`.

Another commonly discussed attack from yesteryear involved a man-in-the-middle (MITM), and was called a smurf attack. Smurf attacks are a good illustration of how spoofing can work, and belong to a type of attack that has recently become more frequent, called an amplification attack.

The middleman is put to good use so that the original source of the attack can't be identified, and the attack's aim is to saturate bandwidth, ultimately causing a denial of service. Worryingly, the barrage of ICMP traffic actually appears to come from the victims themselves. The middleman (also sometimes called the amplifier) receives these spoofed packets and sends a normal echo-response reply to the victim, who didn't even ask for a response. They also have little way of stopping the packets from arriving. Back in the earlier days of the Internet, your ISP could only disable all ICMP traffic to stop the massive flood of data. Because the packets were spoofed, even the logs were of little help in tracking down where they originated.

One solution to this problem is to rate-limit the packets yourself. This leaves ICMP traffic free to arrive, and your network running relatively normally, although possibly a little slower.

This can be achieved on proprietary router hardware, such as Cisco or Juniper, but also on individual hosts by using iptables with a set of rules similar to these:

```
# iptables -I INPUT -p icmp -m limit --limit 30/minute --limit-burst
60 -j ACCEPT
# iptables -I INPUT -p icmp -m limit --limit 6/minute --limit-burst
10 -j LOG
# iptables -I INPUT -p icmp -j DROP
```

From the config shown on the first line, the `--limit-burst` option allows up to 60 packets to arrive initially before the rate limit of one packet every other second is enabled (the 30/minute value). The second line then says that you will log (though much more strictly) how much traffic is accepted before being logged to syslog: six entries per minute after a burst of ten packets. Finally, you'll discard those packets in order to mitigate any effect.

If I'm reading the documentation correctly, the `--limit-burst` value refers back to the specified period used by `--limit`. When that limit is not reached, `--limit-burst` benefits by an increment — in other words, by the value of one — every time the limit isn't reached, up to the number configured.

## Summary

Some of the changes you have explored can be damaging to both systems and networks. You should know what you're doing (and ideally, experiment on a test machine) before trying any of these settings in production. As mentioned, the classic mistake of becoming panicked by the bad reputation that ICMP has and simply banning all mentions of the protocol on your network is ill-advised.

You have looked at attacks and how to prevent them from affecting the normal operations of your network and servers. You also looked at rate-limiting inbound ICMP traffic.

In addition, you looked at the logging of pings and traceroutes to pick up any recces taking place with nefarious intent on your server, and more importantly, how to safely log these unwanted probes to a file so that an attack won't fill your disks with sizable log files.

It's safe to say that some of this knowledge may only be needed rarely, but the next time someone mentions that they're blocking all ICMP traffic on their server, you can give them a knowing look and say that you're confident that ICMP issues will no longer cause you problems.

# Nmap's Prodigious NSE

Even novice sysadmins have probably heard of and run port scans against local and remote hosts. They may also have heard of one famous port scanner on the market, created by the Nmap Project, called Nmap. Nmap stands for "Network Mapper," and along with being superfast, sophisticated, and efficient, it's brimming with features.

Among its many features, you can test for which operating system a remote server is running, audit the security of both local and remote machines, and create an inventory of the machines and their active services on a network.

You may have used Nmap for port scanning in the past, but there's a good chance that you didn't realize what a powerful penetration-testing tool it is. This is partly thanks to its sophisticated built-in scripting engine. Before you look at that, however, you will first review Nmap's basic port scanning functionality. Then you will learn how Nmap can be used for more advanced white hat activities.

## Basic Port Scanning

Even the basic (port scanning) features bundled with Nmap include advanced options such as spoofing your source IP address (using the -S option). A magnificent selection of features is available. But first, let's start with installing the package.

To install Nmap on Red Hat derivatives, you can use this command:

```
# yum install nmap
```

On Debian and its derivative distributions, you can use this command:

```
# apt-get install nmap
```

If you want to use RPM Package Managers on Red Hat's derivatives rather than running these commands, then you can find more information at https://nmap.org/book/inst-linux.html.

If you're familiar with the file /etc/services on Unix-type machines, then the inclusion of the /usr/share/nmap/nmap-services file with Nmap should make sense. Be aware that your file's location may change slightly. Within this file, you tie port numbers to humanly readable service names — a little like localized DNS, I suppose (like the /etc/hosts file where there's usually a key:value format). One line in the Nmap version of that file would look something like this:

```
Service name    Portnum/protocol   Open-frequency   Optional comments
ftp                 21/sctp                 0.000000              # File
Transfer [Control]
```

```
ftp                      21/tcp                  0.197667
# File Transfer [Control]
ftp                      21/udp                  0.004844              #
File Transfer [Control]
ssh                      22/sctp                 0.000000              #
Secure Shell Login
ssh                      22/tcp                  0.182286              #
Secure Shell Login
ssh                      22/udp                  0.003905              #
Secure Shell Login
telnet                   23/tcp                  0.221265
telnet                   23/udp                  0.006211
```

This file is useful because you can edit it to suit your Nmap activities without accidentally misconfiguring your local machine's /etc/services file. The custom version that Nmap includes also adds a little more detail to the usual two fields in your local file. As you can see in this example, there are four columns with field descriptions at the top.

Some people call this port mapping, which isn't a bad description. If you're curious, the open-frequency field has been populated following extensive research online (by running a large number of Nmap scans) and tells you how often the study found that port to be open. This more comprehensive configuration file can also be a useful reference when you're trying to troubleshoot an issue.

What about asking Nmap to run a simple scan on a machine? Let's perform a basic port scan on a remote IPv4 IP address. In this example you use the "-PN" option in order to miss out a ping test, assuming you know that the machine is online (note that older versions of Nmap used "-P0" and "-PN", in case it causes confusion, and stands for "host discovery"):

```
# nmap -PN 123.123.123.123
```

The results might look something like this:

```
Starting Nmap 5.51 ( http://nmap.org ) at 2016-11-16 11:16 GMT
Nmap scan report for www.chrisbinnie.tld (123.123.123.123)
Host is up (0.00051s latency).
Not shown: 999 closed ports
PORT     STATE SERVICE
22/tcp   open  ssh
Nmap done: 1 IP address (1 host up) scanned in 0.09 seconds
```

You can see that 999 ports were scanned by default, without you asking Nmap to look at any others, and only the SSH port was listening on your remote host.

As you might expect, you can scan a whole network as follows:

```
# nmap -PN 123.123.123.0/24
```

By including -n in the options, you can disable DNS lookups to potentially speed up your results and avoid detection by DNS servers, which would otherwise serve the answers to your queries.

If it's TCP that you're interested in, then Nmap can connect to TCP ports as follows:

```
# nmap -sT www.chrisbinnie.tld
```

Simply swap -sT to -sU for UDP ports if they're of interest.

As I've mentioned, there are simply too many options to cover, but before you get to the really good stuff, here are a couple of other options that I find useful.

First, if you're scanning your local network but don't want to include certain hosts, then you can use an exclude file option like this:

```
# nmap 10.10.10.0/24 --excludefile /home/chrisbinnie/exclusions.txt
```

If there are just a few servers that you need to ignore, then you can opt to use the following syntax:

```
# nmap 10.10.10.0/24 --exclude 10.10.10.1,10.10.10.10, 10.10.10.100
```

For scanning specific port numbers, you prepend U for UDP and T for TCP as follows:

```
# nmap -p U:53,T:0-1024,8080 10.10.10.111
```

Finally, if you want to see which hosts are up and running on your local network, then this is the command to choose (it's using a "discovery" or ping scan, hence the P):

```
# nmap -sP 10.10.10.0/24
```

You would expect an output similar to this:

```
Nmap scan report for mail.chrisbinnie.tld (10.10.10.10)
Host is up (0.028s latency).
Nmap scan report for smtp.chrisbinnie.tld (10.10.10.11)
Host is up (0.029s latency).
```

In other words, one line per host.

# The Nmap Scripting Engine

Nmap has a highly sophisticated set of technological innards. It refers to its scripting engine as NSE (Nmap Scripting Engine). I'll run through some of the subjects covered in its extensive documentation and indicate when you may want to use some of its functionality.

The extraordinary NSE was designed with a few key functions in mind. These functions include network discovery mostly through port scanning, advanced service detection using a variety of predefined signatures, vulnerability checking (and exploitation), and finally backdoor detection.

NSE's strength is in its versatility, and it extends this functionality by offering the addition, as its name would suggest, of scripts that can be written by anyone using the Lua programming language. In order to fire up NSE from the command line, you simply launch the nmap binary with the --script= option or, alternatively, the -sC option.

Following are two examples of port scanning with Nmap. The first is without enabling NSE and the second engages it. This should be useful so that you can familiarize yourself with the difference in output. In Listing 7.1 you see the results of the first command. Note that both these commands are run, not as the root user, but as a standard user.

**LISTING 7.1   Nmap performing network discovery but without NSE being engaged**

```
# nmap -p0-1024 -T4 localhost
Starting Nmap 5.51 ( http://nmap.org ) at 2016-11-16 11:16 GMT
Nmap scan report for localhost (127.0.0.1)
Host is up (0.00049s latency).
Not shown: 1021 closed ports
PORT     STATE SERVICE
22/tcp   open  ssh
25/tcp   open  smtp
80/tcp   open  http
111/tcp  open  rpcbind
Nmap done: 1 IP address (1 host up) scanned in 0.11 seconds
```

In Listing 7.2, however, you see that NSE has been engaged, and here it adds invaluable insight into the mix.

**LISTING 7.2   The richer output provided by network discovery with NSE being engaged**

```
# nmap -sC -p0-1024 -T4 localhost
Starting Nmap 5.51 ( http://nmap.org ) at 2016-11-16 11:16 GMT
Nmap scan report for localhost (127.0.0.1)
Host is up (0.00054s latency).
Not shown: 1021 closed ports
PORT     STATE SERVICE
22/tcp   open  ssh
| ssh-hostkey: 1024 d7:46:46:2d:fc:ad:9e:c7:25:d3:a1:96:45:4f:59:d9 (DSA)
|_2048 80:f2:29:c0:ee:a1:80:99:2e:7f:26:c3:b1:2d:c4:37 (RSA)
```

```
25/tcp  open   smtp
80/tcp  open   http
| http-methods: Potentially risky methods: TRACE
|_See http://nmap.org/nsedoc/scripts/http-methods.html
|_http-title: Site doesn't have a title (text/html; charset=UTF-8).
111/tcp open   rpcbind
Nmap done: 1 IP address (1 host up) scanned in 0.16 seconds
```

In Listing 7.2 you can see the additional input from NSE. In contrast to Listing 7.1, you also receive URLs to further research your findings, more host detail (such as the SSH host key in this case), and even comments about the HTML that Nmap doesn't think is valid HTML.

## Timing Templates

In Listings 7.1 and 7.2, you asked for information about ports in the 0-to-1,024 range (the privileged, raw, or superuser ports on Unix-type systems) by using the -p0-1024 option. The -T4 option isn't actually a timeout value of four seconds but instead offers a way of pulling up a specific timing template used by NSE. The higher the setting, the faster Nmap runs, and the values that are available range from 0 to 5.

The timing template values are important and can make a difference to your emotional well-being. These values, from 0 to 5, stand for paranoid, sneaky, polite, normal, aggressive, and insane. The words can also be used in place of the numbers if you find them easier to remember.

Because so many settings were bundled with NSE, the main programmer realized that users might get lost in their complexity, and so introduced templates that might be helpful.

The main reason that the templates are so important to using Nmap is that when you run NSE against a lot of hosts, or a large network or networks, the process can take a very long time to complete. You may also discover very little interesting information (because of well-configured firewalls), and your task can still take what seems like forever to complete.

What's the difference in the templates, you may ask? Both the paranoid and sneaky templates offer some degree of avoiding detection by an intrusion detection system (IDS). The polite template slows down the scanning process in order to limit the bandwidth used at both ends of the connection and also the target machine's resources. The -T3 switch actually does nothing whatsoever; that's because the normal template is the default and is switched on anyway. The aggressive template, which you used with the -T4 switch in the earlier example, will speed up the scanning process and test a relatively high-capacity network's limits more rigorously. The last template, insane, assumes that you are happy to trade off some accuracy in the results that NSE provides against the time it takes to execute. You should have a high-capacity and reliable network if you want to use this setting.

# Categorizing Scripts

Despite employing a highly sophisticated underlying engine, NSE was so thoughtfully designed that even a new user can understand how to operate it with relative ease. It's therefore possible to deploy NSE promptly and without requiring too much reading in advance.

However, to avoid getting ahead of yourself, it's useful to know how NSE refers to the different scripts that it uses. When you run a script through NSE, a port scan will usually be performed prior to or during its execution in order to check the current state of a target machine's network availability. There are also other similarities among the many NSE scripts, such as DNS lookups and traceroutes.

In Table 7.1 you can see how NSE categorizes its scripts; there are a number of different categories to consider.

**TABLE 7.1** **The Script Categories That Come with NSE**

| Category | Description |
| --- | --- |
| auth | These scripts look at authentication methods and circumventing them — for example, x11-access, ftp-anon, and oracle-enum-users. The brute category is for brute forcing and not authentication. |
| broadcast | If you need to broadcast on the local network, employ this bundle of scripts. |
| brute | For brute forcing the authentication credentials of a remote host, use this collection of scripts. There are many available for different protocols. |
| default | The default scripts are executed if you use the -sC or -A options. To use specific scripts, override the default with --script=. |
| discovery | To track who and what is connected to a network, these scripts are all about examining, for example, public registries, SNMP-enabled devices, and directory services. |
| dos | If you want to test a vulnerability or (carefully) run scripts that have the possibility of crashing services, then this set is suitable for your denial-of-service needs. |
| exploit | In order to try out an exploit to see if it succeeds, these scripts will do exactly that. |
| external | Be warned that by executing these scripts, your actions may be logged by other parties. That's because this set of scripts might perform a third-party query, such as a WHOIS lookup, and you would be visible to that WHOIS service. |
| fuzzer | These scripts will search for software bugs and security holes by injecting randomized fields into their queries while you perform your search. They take much longer than other techniques to knock a server offline or find anything of interest. |

| Category | Description |
|----------|-------------|
| intrusive | Ostracized to this unpleasant category, these scripts are very risky to run and won't make it to the safe category. Some of the risks include crashes, bandwidth saturation, and being spotted by sysadmins on target machines. |
| malware | Known malware leaves certain system traces, such as backdoors or signs of infection. Unusual port numbers and service oddities are searched for with malware scripts. |
| safe | This set of scripts is less likely to offend the sysadmins of target systems. Still, you shouldn't completely rely on these scripts not to cause problems. |
| version | You can't select these scripts directly because they are an extension to NSE's version detection functionality. They execute if the version detection option (-sV) is used. |
| vuln | If vulnerabilities are discovered, then this set will alert you about them; otherwise, little noise will be made. Examples are `realvnc-auth-bypass` and `afp-path-vuln`. |

7

## Contributing Factors

When the default set of scripts is used, you might be surprised at how the mighty NSE reaches its decisions. There are no set thresholds; rather, it reaches a kind of score after running through the following criteria.

- *Speed* — default scans must be completed swiftly, for example, so no brute forcing is employed.

- *Usefulness* — if a script doesn't produce useful results, then you can forget its inclusion in default scripts.

- *Verbosity* — the resulting output of running a script needs to be succinct. Equally, when there's nothing to report, silence is a virtue.

- *Reliability* — inevitably, assumptions and guesses are made during the operation of some scripts. However, if there are frequently errors, then it shouldn't be run in the default category.

- *Intrusiveness* — if a script causes armed guards to suddenly appear, then it's probably too intrusive for the default set of scripts.

- *Privacy* — along the same line as the external set of scripts, the default scripts need to respect your privacy and not reveal your presence.

## Security Holes

Now that you've looked at the multitude of NSE's script categories and you also appreciate what running the default set of scripts means, let's look at performing some penetration testing using your new-found knowledge and the abundance of bundled scripts that come with Nmap as standard.

Let's first run a vulnerability check on your local machine as follows:

```
# nmap --script vuln localhost
```

In Listing 7.3 you can see the output from that command, noting that you only engaged the vulnerability scripts using the `vuln` option.

**LISTING 7.3   The direct vulnerability scan made worrisome reading.**

```
Starting Nmap 5.51 ( http://nmap.org ) at 2016-11-16 11:16 GMT
Nmap scan report for localhost (127.0.0.1)
Host is up (0.00090s latency).
Not shown: 996 closed ports
PORT     STATE SERVICE
22/tcp   open  ssh
25/tcp   open  smtp
80/tcp   open  http
| http-enum:
|_  /icons/: Potentially interesting folder w/ directory listing
111/tcp open  rpcbind
Nmap done: 1 IP address (1 host up) scanned in 1.18 seconds
```

The results in Listing 7.3 immediately caught my interest when I saw "Potentially interesting folder" for the RPC service. Of course, it's possible that only my local machine can query the /icons/ folder to which it is referring, but there's also a chance that this needs to be looked into (and relatively urgently). You might firewall off TCP port 111 entirely or shut down the service to remedy such a find unless you're aware of config rules limiting access to RPC.

Rather than hunting for config files, my first test to remedy this issue would be to use netcat to query TCP port 111 from another machine to see if it responds. (The more modern ncat, also written by the Nmap Project, is my preferred version, or if that's unavailable, the telnet command.)

Incidentally, if NSE identifies a known vulnerability, then you would hopefully receive a patch ID for Windows servers or some other relevant URL so that you could research it further. This can save time researching exploits via online searching. There's a good chance that if NSE flags a positive, then a few different tests have been satisfied to reach that conclusion, and unlike some other tools, you shouldn't dismiss its findings without checking them first.

# Authentication Checks

Let's consider what the results would be if someone else ran Nmap's NSE against my local machine, looking for authentication issues. Clearly my local machine has looser permissions (when speaking to itself and not a remote host), but this way of testing still has educational merit. The following command does exactly that and looks for auth script hits:

```
# nmap --script auth localhost
```

The results of this command reveal some of the tests that NSE has run, as you can see in Listing 7.4.

**LISTING 7.4  My auth scripts have been put to work, again on my local machine.**

```
Starting Nmap 5.51 ( http://nmap.org ) at 2016-11-16 11:16 GMT
Nmap scan report for localhost (127.0.0.1)
Host is up (0.00062s latency).
Not shown: 996 closed ports
PORT    STATE SERVICE
22/tcp  open  ssh
25/tcp  open  smtp
80/tcp  open  http
| http-brute:
|_  ERROR: No path was specified (see http-brute.path)
|_citrix-brute-xml: FAILED: No domain specified (use ntdomain argument)
| http-form-brute:
|_  ERROR: No uservar was specified (see http-form-brute.uservar)
| http-domino-enum-passwords:
|_  ERROR: No valid credentials were found (see domino-enum-passwords.
    username and domino-enum-passwords.password)
111/tcp open  rpcbind
Nmap done: 1 IP address (1 host up) scanned in 0.17 seconds
```

Looking at the results displayed underneath the port numbers in Listing 7.4, you can see that Nmap clearly wants some more information (from varying inputs) and has generated three ERROR messages in the meantime. You might see some user accounts that NSE has discovered, displayed under a section such as "Host script results" at the end of such an output if usernames were gleaned from executing such a request, for example, against a Windows domain.

# Discovery

Consider the following command, to provide you with more information about a host:

```
# nmap --script discovery localhost
```

**LISTING 7.5  You have discovered a lot of useful information about your localhost.**

```
Starting Nmap 5.51 ( http://nmap.org ) at 2016-11-16 11:16 GMT
Nmap scan report for localhost (127.0.0.1)
Host is up (0.00070s latency).
Not shown: 996 closed ports
PORT    STATE SERVICE
22/tcp  open  ssh
|_banner: SSH-2.0-OpenSSH_5.3
| ssh-hostkey: 1024 d7:46:46:2d:fc:ad:9e:c7:25:d3:a1:96:45:4f:59:d9 (DSA)
|_2048 80:f2:29:c0:ee:a1:80:99:2e:7f:26:c3:b1:2d:c4:37 (RSA)
25/tcp  open  smtp
|_banner: 220 mail.chrisbinnie.tld ESMTP Postfix
| smtp-enum-users:
|   root
|   admin
|_  Method RCPT returned a unhandled status code.
|_smtp-open-relay: Server is an open relay (16/16 tests)
80/tcp  open  http
| http-headers:
|   Date: Mon, 16 Nov 2015 11:37:52 GMT
|   Server: Apache/2.2.15 (Red Hat)
|   Last-Modified: Mon, 15 Jun 2015 13:57:09 GMT
|   ETag: "4bc-61-5188ed5743e6a"
|   Accept-Ranges: bytes
|   Content-Length: 97
|   Connection: close
|   Content-Type: text/html; charset=UTF-8
|
|_  (Request type: HEAD)
|_http-title: Site doesn't have a title (text/html; charset=UTF-8).
|_http-date: Mon, 16 Nov 2015 11:37:52 GMT; 0s from local time.
| http-vhosts:
|_393 names had status 200
| http-enum:
|_  /icons/: Potentially interesting folder w/ directory listing
```

```
111/tcp open   rpcbind
| rpcinfo:
|   100000  2,3,4           111/tcp  rpcbind
|_  100000  2,3,4           111/udp  rpcbind
Nmap done: 1 IP address (1 host up) scanned in 11.51 seconds
```

In Listing 7.5 you are blessed with the ability to retrieve HTTP headers, SMTP banners, and RPC issues, among other things, via the discovery scripts. Although the SMTP error "Server is an open relay (16/16 tests)" is present, it's likely a false positive but definitely worth checking so that you're certain.

With all of these included features, this mode is highly useful and represents a key part of NSE's functionality. After all, you can't exploit services without knowing they exist. From the results generated by NSE, it is safe to say that, when it comes to discovering machines and services, information is power. The sophisticated NSE doesn't bombard you with too much detail, however, just enough to be useful.

The negative impact of running scripts by category is that it can slightly reduce performance if you include all the scripts in a category. However, it does mean that you're not relying on the scoring system used by the default set of scripts or executing all the scripts available to a template type. You can be much more focused if you're just looking for a specific type of information, however.

# Updating Scripts

As you might imagine, the custom scripts written for NSE using the Lua language are frequently improved and augmented. If you want to update your NSE scripts, you can do so selectively by downloading and copying them into a directory, similar to this path, on Unix-type systems:

```
/usr/share/nmap/scripts
```

If you add or remove scripts from the scripts directory or if you have changed a script's category, then you need to run the following command (as the root user) afterwards:

```
# nmap --script-updatedb
```

The output will hopefully be something like this:

```
Starting Nmap 5.51 ( http://nmap.org ) at 2016-11-16 11:16 GMT
NSE: Updating rule database.
NSE: Script Database updated successfully.
Nmap done: 0 IP addresses (0 hosts up) scanned in 0.14 seconds
```

To download scripts from the Nmap website, you can click the Scripts link in the Categories panel at https://nmap.org/nsedoc/lib/nmap.html.

At the time of writing, there are over 500 eye-watering scripts to consider, each with information relating to their functionality.

# Script Type

It is worth mentioning that within the underlying infrastructure of NSE, there are four supported script types:

- *Prerule scripts* - as you'd guess, these are run at the start and before any scanning begins. For example, you might want to perform reverse DNS lookups on a list of IP addresses before examining them.
- *Host scripts* - during standard scanning processes (that is, after discovery, port scanning, version detection, and operating system detection), these scripts are run on the target.
- *Service scripts* - if NSE identifies a service, it can then execute these scripts against it. For example, there are more than 15 HTTP scripts to run against web servers.
- *Postrule scripts* - these are run once NSE has finished its scanning tasks, and they tend to concentrate on how results are output. As I've said, brevity is important, as verbosity can cause confusion.

The comprehensive Nmap documentation (found at https://nmap.org) makes the point of explaining that "[m]any scripts could potentially run as either a prerule or postrule script. In those cases, we recommend using a prerule for consistency."

# Regular Expressions

The clever command line with which NSE is familiar can also cope with regular expressions (regex). For example, I mentioned the 15 HTTP scripts; to trigger all of these scripts in one run, you might run a command against a target web server such as this:

```
# nmap --script "http-*"
```

You can also make Boolean decisions as follows (just as you'd expect with regex):

```
# nmap --script "default or safe"
```

Hopefully this command is easy enough to understand. The documentation also presents this more complex example:

```
# nmap --script "(default or safe or intrusive) and not http-*"
```

Here you can see that you want to enable the default, safe, and intrusive script categories, but not those that deal with web servers.

# Graphical User Interfaces

As an aside, you can also save the output (which if it's lengthy would usually scroll rapidly up your console) to file in the usual way, as you can in this example, Unix-style:

```
# nmap -sC -p0-1024 -T4 localhost > /home/chrisbinnie/output.txt
```

However, the NSE way to save the output is as follows, outputting to plain text:

```
# nmap -T5 localhost -o outputfile.txt
```

You can also output information to XML as follows:

```
# nmap -T5 localhost -oX outputfile.xml
```

# Zenmap

There are times, especially if you're dealing with many target machines across different networks, that you need some help with your results. Imagine being able to add your results to a database so that you can search for common patterns with ease across historical scans.

Step forward, Zenmap (https://nmap.org/zenmap/). The official GUI scanner for Nmap, the well-designed Zenmap is also free and appropriate for users of all levels. A command creator is included to assist in making up complex commands and the ability to perform historical searching via a database. It's also possible to create profiles for commonly run commands so you're not continually retyping them.

This highly useful graphical cross-platform tool is available for Linux, BSD, Mac OS, and Windows, among other systems.

Another nice feature is that you can run a diff and then compare the results of two scans in order to more easily discover what happened between then and now.

For users who frequently perform scans, and indeed any user who is new to security, Zenmap should be the tool of choice. Users of all experience levels should find the learning curve considerably less steep by using Zenmap first. Figure 7.1 shows what you can expect from using the graphical Zenmap on a Desktop Manager in Linux.

**FIGURE 7.1**

An example of Zenmap at work, as found at the Zenmap homepage (https://nmap.org/zenmap/)

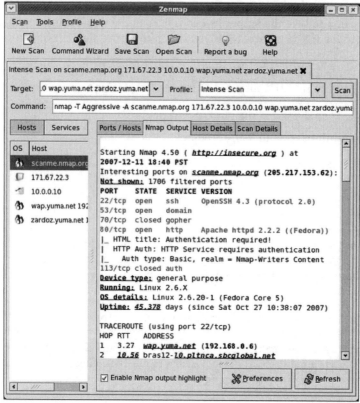

*Copyright 2015 Insecure.Com LLC*

# Summary

In this chapter, I've touched on just some of Nmap's basic functionality, introduced and explained the different script categories of NSE, discussed the types of scripts that Nmap can use, and explored using a GUI to take the initial complexity away from repetitive tasks. Of course, I would be remiss not to mention again that the GUI also helps with analysis.

There are hundreds of options, as well as white hat and black hat scenarios, that Nmap supports and encourages you to experiment with. It's important to learn how attackers might approach your system, but equally to use these powerful tools with care and respect.

After all, bringing down other people's servers is no fun. It's stopping other people from bringing down your servers that is a bigger challenge, and as a result it's much more satisfying (and completely legal).

7

# Malware Detection

The term *malware* encompasses a large range of unwelcome software that is designed to damage a computer. A partial list of malware might, for example, include viruses, spyware, Trojan horses, and worms. The rapid proliferation of such software is enough to concern users of all levels, from novices to seasoned administrators. The impact of malware ranges from essentially harmless pranks to the theft of personal information, such as banking details, or a denial of service.

Although the level of scaremongering in the news ebbs and flows, every good sysadmin knows that there's no such thing as a completely secure system. Despite the massive number of virus and malware threats that target Windows machines, all users of Unix-type machines should remember that these threats also exist for their systems.

One popular, sophisticated software package called Linux Malware Detect (LMD), from R-fx Networks (`https://www.rfxn.com`), helps to mitigate malware threats on Linux systems. Let's look at how you can effectively protect Linux machines against malware using the LMD package, which only focuses on malware, unlike other more diluted solutions.

## Getting Started

Before we begin with looking at LMD itself, let's consider some potentially less obvious aspects of what's needed to successfully keep your malware software functioning correctly.

### Definition Update Frequency

It is critical that malware signature updates be performed frequently; in fact, your system may be vulnerable if you have missed the latest update. The architecture of the detection software itself is of little value if current threats are not detected. Fortunately, LMD frequently pulls in its updates, from which it generates signatures, from community data, user submissions, and the firewall data of active malware threats.

The LMD website offers an up-to-date RSS feed of the latest threats, and also provides a commercial version, which is another incentive for updates to be current and relevant. The feed, which is brimming with LMD's current malware findings, can be found at `https://www.rfxn.com/feed/`.

LMD states that signatures receive an update approximately once a day, or more often if a flurry of activity is reported.

## Malware Hash Registry

A well-respected security website called Team Cymru provides a Malware Hash Registry (www.team-cymru.org/MHR.html), which provides a lookup service to compare malware infections. According to LMD, over 30 major antivirus companies use this data to populate their databases. From the LMD website, you can see the current number of reported threats as follows:

```
DETECTED KNOWN MALWARE: 1951
% AV DETECT (AVG): 58
% AV DETECT (LOW): 10
% AV DETECT (HIGH): 100
UNKNOWN MALWARE: 6931
```

The LMD website then continues and explores some of the scoring used to measure successful hits and misses by other malware products, resulting in a worrying conclusion.

> Using the Team Cymru malware hash registry, we can see that of the 8,883 malware hashes shipping with LMD 1.5, ... 6,931 or 78% of threats ... went undetected by 30 commercial anti-virus and malware products. The 1,951 threats that were detected had an average detection rate of 58% with a low and high detection rate of 10% and 100% respectively. There could not be a clearer statement to the need for an open and community driven malware remediation project that focuses on the threat landscape of multi-user shared environments.

As you can see from this LMD website excerpt, there are a significant number of failures among commercial malware products. LMD aims to plug the market gap where possible, but is an advocate of open discussions and collaboration, sharing known threat details between vendors.

## Prevalent Threats

At the time of writing, LMD claims to hold 10,822 malware signatures within its database. Looking at the contents of Figure 8.1, you can see a list of the top 60 most prevalent threats within the LMD database. As you might expect, the world's most popular server-side scripting language, PHP (https://www.php.net), is a common attack vector. The powerful Perl language also features heavily.

## LMD Features

The LMD feature set is far from trivial. In Figure 8.2 you can see the features listed in its documentation.

**FIGURE 8.1**

The top 60 most prevalent attacks according to LMD

```
base64.inject.unclassed      perl.ircbot.xscan
bin.dccserv.irsexxy          perl.mailer.yellsoft
bin.fakeproc.Xnuxer          perl.shell.cbLorD
bin.ircbot.nbot              perl.shell.cgitelnet
bin.ircbot.php3              php.cmdshell.c100
bin.ircbot.unclassed         php.cmdshell.c99
bin.pktflood.ABC123          php.cmdshell.cih
bin.pktflood.osf             php.cmdshell.egyspider
bin.trojan.linuxsmalli       php.cmdshell.fx29
c.ircbot.tsunami             php.cmdshell.ItsmYarD
exp.linux.rstb               php.cmdshell.Ketemu
exp.linux.unclassed          php.cmdshell.N3tshell
exp.setuid0.unclassed        php.cmdshell.r57
gzbase64.inject              php.cmdshell.unclassed
html.phishing.auc61          php.defash.buno
html.phishing.hsbc           php.exe.globals
perl.connback.DataCha0s      php.include.remote
perl.connback.N2             php.ircbot.InsideTeam
perl.cpanel.cpwrap           php.ircbot.lolwut
perl.ircbot.atrixteam        php.ircbot.sniper
perl.ircbot.bRuNo            php.ircbot.vj_denie
perl.ircbot.Clx              php.mailer.10hack
perl.ircbot.devil            php.mailer.bombam
perl.ircbot.fx29             php.mailer.PostMan
perl.ircbot.magnum           php.phishing.AliKay
perl.ircbot.oldwolf          php.phishing.mrbrain
perl.ircbot.putr4XtReme      php.phishing.ReZulT
perl.ircbot.rafflesia        php.pktflood.oey
perl.ircbot.UberCracker      php.shell.rc99
perl.ircbot.xdh              php.shell.shellcomm
```

**FIGURE 8.2**

The sizeable list of features that LMD offers

```
.: 2 [ FEATURES ]

- MD5 file hash detection for quick threat identification
- HEX based pattern matching for identifying threat variants
- statistical analysis component for detection of obfuscated threats (e.g: base64)
- integrated detection of ClamAV to use as scanner engine for improved performance
- integrated signature update feature with -u|--update
- integrated version update feature with -d|--update-ver
- scan-recent option to scan only files that have been added/changed in X days
- scan-all option for full path based scanning
- checkout option to upload suspected malware to rfxn.com for review / hashing
- full reporting system to view current and previous scan results
- quarantine queue that stores threats in a safe fashion with no permissions
- quarantine batching option to quarantine the results of a current or past scans
- quarantine restore option to restore files to original path, owner and perms
- quarantine suspend account option to Cpanel suspend or shell revoke users
- cleaner rules to attempt removal of malware injected strings
- cleaner batching option to attempt cleaning of previous scan reports
- cleaner rules to remove base64 and gzinflate(base64 injected malware
- daily cron based scanning of all changes in last 24h in user homedirs
- daily cron script compatible with stock RH style systems, Cpanel & Ensim
- kernel based inotify real time file scanning of created/modified/moved files
- kernel inotify monitor that can take path data from STDIN or FILE
- kernel inotify monitor convenience feature to monitor system users
- kernel inotify monitor can be restricted to a configurable user html root
- kernel inotify monitor with dynamic sysctl limits for optimal performance
- kernel inotify alerting through daily and/or optional weekly reports
- HTTP upload scanning through mod_security2 inspectFile hook
- e-mail alert reporting after every scan execution (manual & daily)
- path, extension and signature based ignore options
- background scanner option for unattended scan operations
- verbose logging & output of all actions
```

8

You can tell that in addition to its clever threat detection, LMD manages to combine comprehensive reporting and the quarantining of threats, among many other features. The ability to receive summary reports on a daily basis through e-mail via a cron job is clearly useful to make sure the detection system is running as expected. In addition, LMD's ability to plug into Apache and directly monitor file uploads from users is something that I will touch on later. If this is the only way that a user can get files onto a system, then it is clearly a bulletproof choice.

## Monitoring Filesystems

One modern method of watching for changes on filesystems is by using inotify. You need a compatible kernel for this functionality to work correctly. Fear not, because inotify is reportedly included in kernels from version 2.6.13 and after, so most Linux builds will have this capability.

The sophisticated inotify can monitor, in real time, both single files and entire directories for changes, alerting configured software if any changes are discovered. If a piece of user-space software is caught making changes, then inotify will consider it an event and report it immediately.

By creating a watch list, inotify can keep track of unique watch descriptors that it associates to each item on its watch list. Although inotify won't pass on details about the user or process that has changed a file or directory, the fact that a change has taken place is enough to satisfy most applications. If inotify isn't available, then the older approach of polling a filesystem or manually running scans will usually apply. In the case of checking for changes on networked filesystems, any configured software will need to resort to polling the filesystem using a predetermined frequency. This is because remote filesystems are harder to keep track of.

Unfortunately, the pseudo filesystems, which include /proc, /sys, and /dev/pts, aren't visible to inotify. This shouldn't be of too much concern, however, because "real" files don't exist in these paths, but rather the ephemeral workings of a system, which change frequently.

## Installation

Let's now look at installing LMD on both Debian and Red Hat derivatives. First, you will check that the wget package is installed with the following command on Red Hat:

```
# yum install wget
```

The alternative on Debian is the following command:

```
# apt-get install wget
```

Many distributions include wget by default, so this may not be needed.

To get the most out of LMD, you can also install `inotify-tools` if you want LMD to interface with inotify directly; you can read more and also download `inotify-tools` from `https://github.com/rvoicilas/inotify-tools/wiki`.

However, to install it from your package manager, if you're lucky and using an offspring of Red Hat, you can use the following command:

```
# yum install inotify-tools
```

And, for machines following Debian's lineage, you should be able to run the following command:

```
# apt-get install inotify-tools
```

If that doesn't work on your Debian flavor, try the following procedure. I know this works because I wanted to see how easy LMD would be to install on Ubuntu 14.04 LTS. I needed to add the Universe repository, in order to successfully install the `inotify-tools` package to my `/etc/apt/sources.list` file, as follows:

```
deb http://us.archive.ubuntu.com/ubuntu trusty main universe
```

You can swap the word "trusty" with "precise" or another Ubuntu release code name if you are running other flavors. You can then update your package lists with the following command:

```
# apt-get update
```

Then, the final Ubuntu command would simply be as follows:

```
# apt-get install inotify-tools
```

I will leave you to experiment with Debian repositories in the same way (replacing "trusty" with your Debian version name).

Because the LMD package itself is not found in package repositories as of this writing, you can download and install the package as follows:

```
# cd /usr/local/src/
# wget http://www.rfxn.com/downloads/maldetect-current.tar.gz
# tar -xzf maldetect-current.tar.gz
# cd maldetect-*
# sh ./install.sh
```

Once you've run the `install.sh` script, as shown on the last line of these commands, you should be presented with output containing content that includes the following:

```
Linux Malware Detect v1.5
            (C) 2002-2015, R-fx Networks <proj@r-fx.org>
            (C) 2015, Ryan MacDonald <ryan@r-fx.org>
```

```
This program may be freely redistributed under the terms of the GNU GPL
installation completed to /usr/local/maldetect
config file: /usr/local/maldetect/conf.maldet
exec file: /usr/local/maldetect/maldet
exec link: /usr/local/sbin/maldet
exec link: /usr/local/sbin/lmd
cron.daily: /etc/cron.daily/maldet
maldet(6617): {sigup} performing signature update check...
maldet(6617): {sigup} local signature set is version 2015112028602
maldet(6617): {sigup} latest signature set already installed
```

Your chosen installation paths might vary, of course, if you have edited the install.sh script (the inspath variable in particular). As you can see, you also receive a note of how up-to-date your LMD signatures are.

## Monitoring Modes

Now that you have installed your package, let's look at what LMD can monitor for you on a system. A good place to start is if you consider LMD's monitoring modes.

LMD offers a number of monitoring modes that can be configured to check different parts of the filesystem. As you will see, LMD uses the binary executable called Maldet, short for "malware detect."

To monitor a system component, you can use the -m option, also written as --monitor. What LMD can monitor may be broken down into users, files, and paths. The website gives you the following example of how the three modes might look on the command line:

```
# maldet --monitor users
# maldet --monitor /root/monitor_paths
# maldet --monitor /home/mike,/home/ashton
```

By using the first option, --monitor users, LMD will monitor any unique identifiers (UIDs) on the system that are above a minimum UID setting. (The config option that can be set in the config file is called notify_minuid.)

The second monitoring example is a file, spaced by new lines, that can contain the files you want to monitor. In this case, the list of files is located in the file /root/monitor_paths.

For the third option, you could potentially create a very long command line by adding a comma-separated list of filesystem paths to keep an eye on.

Figure 8.3 shows the output from running the following command:

```
# maldet -m /home/ubuntu
```

**FIGURE 8.3**

What you see when you ask LMD to monitor a specific path

```
ubuntu maldetect-1.5 # maldet -m /home/ubuntu
Linux Malware Detect v1.5
            (C) 2002-2015, R-fx Networks <proj@rfxn.com>
            (C) 2015, Ryan MacDonald <ryan@rfxn.com>
This program may be freely redistributed under the terms of the GNU GPL v2

maldet(16624): {mon} added /home/ubuntu to inotify monitoring array
maldet(16624): {mon} starting inotify process on 1 paths, this might take awhile...
maldet(16624): {mon} inotify startup successful (pid: 16723)
maldet(16624): {mon} inotify monitoring log: /usr/local/maldetect/logs/inotify_log
ubuntu maldetect-1.5 # █
```

# Configuration

The main config file for LMD is `/usr/local/maldetect/conf.maldet`. It's well commented and is useful for understanding how LMD prefers to be set up.

One word of warning before you continue, however: the LMD config file doesn't use an asterisk for wildcard characters, but instead, a question mark. Therefore, you should use ? characters instead of * to replace multiple characters in a config option. Other than that minor caveat, it's relatively smooth sailing.

## Exclusions

Let's look at how to set up LMD. The documentation starts you off by asking you to consider the elements of the system that you want to ignore. In the same style as the monitoring modes that you have just looked at, there are files that you can populate to achieve this. Each entry in the following config files should be on its own line.

You can add full file paths, which you don't want to be checked by LMD, to this file: `/usr/local/maldetect/ignore_paths`.

You can also exclude a particular file extension globally by putting an entry like `.jpg` in this file: `/usr/local/maldetect/ignore_file_ext`.

Certain LMD signatures might lead to unnecessary and unhelpful logging entries and alerts for one reason or another. You can disable certain signatures by adding a signature, such as `php.mailer.10hack`, to this file: `/usr/local/maldetect/ignore_sigs`.

The last exclusion option means that you can use sophisticated regular expressions (regex) to match multiple filesystem paths at once. You simply add a list to this file, `/usr/local/maldetect/ignore_inotify`, which uses a format like this:

```
^/home/premium-user-$
```

Clearly, by using regex, the file-matching possibilities are endless, and it can be used to avoid making manual changes to your config whenever a new user is allowed to log in to your server. This regex example hopefully points out that you could name a specific set of users with a username format along the lines of `premium-user-123456`.

## Running from the CLI

The Command Line Interface (CLI) options for LMD are well considered and relatively easy to follow. I will leave you to explore all of them, but you will look at some of the key options now.

As I have already mentioned, the executable binary for LMD is called maldet. Let's begin by running LMD in the background while it checks a particular filesystem path. You can see from this example in the documentation how to run potentially large scans in the background as follows, using -b:

```
# maldet -b -r /home/?/public_html 7
```

In this example, -b is used for background scanning and checking files that have been changed or modified in the last seven days, set by the 7 character being appended. The syntax and optional way of running this command is `--scan-recent PATH DAYS`.

## Reporting

Let's have a quick look at how LMD generates its reports. Figure 8.4 shows a produced report.

**FIGURE 8.4**

A report of a scan from LMD using the maldet --report command

```
HOST:       ubuntu
SCAN ID:    151212-1648.17013
STARTED:    Dec 12 2015 16:48:59 +0000
COMPLETED:  Dec 12 2015 16:49:00 +0000
ELAPSED:    1s [find: 0s]

PATH:          /home/*/public_html
RANGE:         7 days
TOTAL FILES:   1
TOTAL HITS:    0
TOTAL CLEANED: 0

==============================================
Linux Malware Detect v1.5 < proj@rfxn.com >
```

To query specific reports, you need a SCANID. This is a unique reference that can be seen near the top of Figure 8.4, where this command runs to give you a report on the last LMD command that was run:

```
# maldet --report
```

Once you have that ID, you can also manually e-mail the report to yourself as follows:

```
# maldet -e, --report SCANID chris@binnie.tld
```

To query a specific SCANID, with a formatted time stamp included within its name (010116 as the date in this example, and the rest of the name being the time), your command might look like this:

```
# maldet --report 010116-1111.21212
```

These options might also be helpful if used with the --log or -l option:

```
# maldet --log
```

You should see LMD logging events by running this command. In my case, despite having only run a few commands so far, there is a relatively substantial amount of detail on my log file. With that command, you are shown the last fifty lines from the file /usr/local/ maldetect/logs/event_log. You can query that file further if you need to discover information not found in those 50 lines. In my opinion, the level of detail logged by LMD is another indication of a sophisticated, well-written package.

## Quarantining and Cleaning

The documentation makes a point of saying that by default, LMD will not act when it finds evil-looking files. It is therefore important to understand that, in most cases, you need to quarantine your malware manually.

If you're certain that you want to enable automatic quarantining, then it's possible to do so by setting the configuration option quar_hits=1 within the main config file, which resides at /usr/local/maldetect/conf.maldet by default.

If you wanted to quarantine all malware from a specific scan, then you would use the -q option, which is also the same as --quarantine SCANID, as follows:

```
# maldet -q 010116-1111.21212
```

If you feel that you've made a mistake, then you can restore quarantined files from a specific SCANID by using the following command, which is the same as the --restore function:

```
# maldet -s 010116-1111.21212
```

You will see an error such as this one if there's nothing to restore:

```
maldet(18748): {restore} could not find a valid hit list to restore.
```

If you want LMD to try to fix malware infections that it discovers, then you can use the --clean command, which is also written as the -n option. Here is an example command of cleaning malware that you found in a particular SCANID:

```
# maldet -n 010116-1111.21212
```

8

For a cleaning to be considered a success, the resulting scan after cleaning a malware infection must pass without registering a HIT of a problem file.

If you begin to doubt results or you're not sure that your config changes have been picked up correctly, then you can purge all of your existing session data, logs, and temporary files with the following command:

```
# maldet -p
```

The result should be similar to this output:

```
maldet(19219): {glob} logs and quarantine data cleared by user
request (-p)
```

## Updating LMD

As I said from the outset, the updating of LMD's signatures is of paramount importance. To manually run an update, you use the -u command option. In case you're wondering, by doing so you connect to the rfxn.com website to retrieve the data. Try it manually yourself with -u, or its equivalent --update, as follows:

```
# maldet -u
```

The expected output would be similar to this:

```
maldet(19278): {sigup} performing signature update check...
maldet(19278): {sigup} local signature set is version 2015112028602
maldet(19278): {sigup} latest signature set already installed
```

There is also a clever mechanism for updating the currently installed version, again from rfxn.com, as follows:

```
# maldet --update-ver
```

This can also be abbreviated to -d if you want, and the results of this command might look like this:

```
maldet(19357): {update} checking for available updates...
maldet(19357): {update} hashing install files and checking against
server...
maldet(19357): {update} latest version already installed.
```

## Scanning and Stopping Scans

In Figure 8.1 you saw the results of monitoring a particular path with the -m or --monitor option. Let's expand on that for a moment.

Imagine that you want to monitor two particular filesystem partitions, because your users potentially have the ability to write data there. You would monitor the paths as follows:

```
# maldet -m /usr/local,/home
```

Note the comma that is separating the paths. The output for running this command is shown in Figure 8.5. Remember that large scans can use the -b background option, as you saw earlier.

**FIGURE 8.5**

What you see when LMD starts monitoring two filesystem partitions with inotify enabled

```
ubuntu sess # maldet -m /usr/local,/home
Linux Malware Detect v1.5
            (C) 2002-2015, R-fx Networks <proj@rfxn.com>
            (C) 2015, Ryan MacDonald <ryan@rfxn.com>
This program may be freely redistributed under the terms of the GNU GPL v2

maldet(20035): {mon} added /usr/local to inotify monitoring array
maldet(20035): {mon} added /home to inotify monitoring array
maldet(20035): {mon} starting inotify process on 2 paths, this might take awhile...
maldet(20035): {mon} inotify startup successful (pid: 20646)
maldet(20035): {mon} inotify monitoring log: /usr/local/maldetect/logs/inotify_log
ubuntu sess # 
```

Let's consider how to manually scan a directory and its subdirectories without using background mode. Imagine you have users uploading files via FTP or SFTP to an upload directory:

```
# maldet -a /home/?/uploads
```

In this example, you use LMD to scan the uploads directory for all users with a home directory (remember that the question mark is the wildcard character in LMD, not the asterisk).

Having run the scanning command, you are also offered a SCANID for future reference, as you can see from the data it generates:

```
maldet(28566): {scan} scan of /home/*/uploads (1 files) in
progress...
maldet(28566): {scan} 1111/1111 files scanned: 0 hits 0 cleaned
maldet(28566): {scan} scan completed on /home/*/uploads: files 1111,
malware hits 0, cleaned hits 0, time 11s
maldet(28566): {scan} scan report saved, to view run: maldet --report
151212-1724.28566
```

8

If any of your scans take longer than expected, then LMD can accommodate this scenario too. The kill switch or -k option (also written as --kill) will stop any inotify instance in its tracks. If machine load is too high or you think something isn't behaving as it should, then this is a useful addition to the available options.

## Cron Job

LMD comes with a daily cron job, which is located at /etc/cron.daily/maldet. This will update signatures and clean up scan data so that it's kept for up to fourteen days, as well as run a daily scan using the config that you have specified.

Note that session data and temporary files are kept between cron job executions. As a result, you need to run the -p option that I mentioned earlier to purge those files if you think your results aren't accurate.

You should set up the e-mail configuration parameters in order to receive daily reports every morning. The daily update is valuable for e-mail archival reasons and for making sure that your scans are taking place every day and haven't failed.

## Reporting Malware

You've seen how sophisticated and well-constructed LMD is, and it should therefore come as no surprise that LMD provides a simple mechanism for uploading suspicious files for analysis. If they prove to be infected with an unknown variety of malware, then new signatures may be created and added to LMD's known threats in order to identify malware for other users. The method to send files back to LMD for checking is as follows, using the --checkout feature, which is also written as the -c option:

```
# maldet -c suspicious_file.gz
```

When you execute this command, your file will be submitted to rfxn.com and checked in due course.

## Apache Integration

Earlier in the chapter, I briefly alluded to a clever feature that is included with LMD. This feature is the ability to integrate LMD with the Apache mod_security2 module. The LMD documentation explains that it uses the malleable Apache module's inspectFile hook functionality to enable you to run a validation script that can determine if an upload is to pass or fail. So, for example, inside your Apache config file, you might see this entry, taken from the documentation:

```
SecRequestBodyAccess On
SecRule FILES_TMPNAMES "@inspectFile /usr/local/maldetect/hookscan.
sh" \
                "id:'999999',log,auditlog,deny,severity:2,phase:2,t:
none"
```

By design, each upload of a file by a user can be scanned automatically, which should significantly reduce the number of threats on a system, especially where many users are uploading files frequently.

The documentation includes details of how performance and accuracy have been considered in the default options. If you're interested in this feature, then I would encourage you to check out the bundled README file for more information.

# Summary

In addition to looking at LMD, I touched upon the inotify mechanism that it uses to check for filesystem changes in real time. The clever and efficient inotify allows real-time checks for malware without significant system load being introduced.

With Android smartphones currently accounting for over 80 percent of the global market, there is little doubt that the malware written to exploit vulnerabilities in those devices will appear to a greater extent on Linux user devices as well as servers in the future.

By enabling real-time filesystem checks alongside sophisticated tools such as LMD, you should reduce your risk of a malware infection significantly. LMD was initially designed for servers offering shared hosting because the author felt the user-account attack vector was being missed by other products, which usually focused on kernel and rootkit infections.

Having tried installing LMD in a test environment first, however, and having become familiar with how it operates, I believe that LMD is definitely worth considering for use on your production machines.

8

# Password Cracking with Hashcat

Two sophisticated security tools caught my eye recently. They were highlighted in the news because they've been released as open source, apparently causing a frenzy on GitHub as developers looked for the tools' source code. The tools in question are called Hashcat and oclHashcat. Hashcat (https://hashcat.net/hashcat) boldly refers to itself as the "world's fastest CPU-based password recovery tool." Its close relative, oclHashcat, uses your Graphics Processing Unit (GPU) to number crunch its way through the process of recovering passwords, as opposed to Hashcat's CPU-based approach. As a result, the GPU-based oclHashcat is even faster than Hashcat.

While tools like this can be highly useful for legitimately rescuing a lost password, it is also possible to use them for nefarious purposes. It hopefully goes without saying that these powerful tools should be used responsibly. They are employed by forensic scientists and penetration testers, but if you find evidence of similar tools on one of your machines, then you should certainly raise the alarm.

Let's look at how these tools work for saving the day if a password becomes lost, as well as how a hacker will approach attacking your passwords.

## History

Another popular, venerable security tool that is used for ripping passwords is called John the Ripper, and its origins go back many years. Hashcat arrived on the scene in 2009, and took it upon itself to use multithreaded CPU password cracking. At that time, although other tool developers had begun looking at using all the available cores of a CPU, none were able to do so fully and without patching. When the developers were designing Hashcat, it made absolute sense to take advantage of the capabilities of modern CPUs and speed up the password recovery process significantly.

In case it causes confusion, Hashcat originally went through a few different names in its early releases, such as atomcrack and Dr. Hash. As of version 0.30, the name that you know (and I'm sure you will begin to love), Hashcat, was applied to the software.

## Understanding Passwords

It might be helpful to look at how password systems work. I'll use Linux systems as my case in point before continuing onto Hashcat in detail.

## Keyspace

It's important to understand the concept of what keyspace is in cryptography. It loosely relates to how much effort a password-cracking tool will have to expend.

The keyspace is simply the set of available keys that might be used when generating a particular key. The National Institute of Standards and Technology (NIST) describes keyspace as the "total number of possible values that a key, such as a password, can have."

It continues, "A component of keyspace used in common passwords is the 'Character Set' used to make up the key."

In other words, in a password you can only use the available characters on your keyboard (or in your current locale's character set), and they represent a password's keyspace.

Even a single character can have a keyspace of ten characters if that character is a single number, ranging from zero to nine.

You can increase the security of your passwords by increasing both the length of the passwords and the size of your character sets. So, for example, a password with 16 characters that uses a character set sized at 10 characters would reportedly have a keyspace of 10,000,000,000,000,000, making it much harder to attack than the 10-character keyspace from a single character.

This helpful website might encourage you to increase your password security: https://howsecureismypassword.net.

This simple yet sophisticated site uses basic terms and discusses possible combinations as opposed to keyspace. If you click the SHOW DETAILS link under the input box, after you've entered a password, you will see how secure the password is. For example, the following output appeared after I entered a one-character-long password:

```
Length 1 characters
Character Combinations 10
Calculations Per Second 4 billion
Possible Combinations 10
```

Now for the part that should cause you great concern. The powerful password tool on the "How Secure Is My Password" website reports that the cracking time for my single-digit password is roughly 0.0000000025 seconds for a standard desktop computer. Imagine how fast it might be if you combined the processing capacity of many video cards.

Trying to be a little more clever, by contrast, you can see what happens when I enter a 16-character password in the example that follows. Incidentally, I'm using my computer's default character set, so here the 10-character-long character set example that you just looked at won't apply.

The password I entered was a combination of upper and lower alpha characters, numeric, and special characters, as follows:

```
Rx951&RTdIp-"2YT
```

In this case the website responded with a more comforting time to crack, of 412 trillion years. As you can see in the following output, some new vocabulary is included (for me, at least). Apparently, the word "nonillion" is a number followed by 30 zeros in the United States and 54 zeros in the United Kingdom.

```
Length 16 characters
Character Combinations 96
Calculations Per Second 4 billion
Possible Combinations 52 nonillion
```

From this example, you can clearly surmise that a standard eight-character-long "complicated" password is preferable to using a simple single-character password.

## Hashes

Now that I've covered how a complex password can dramatically increase the effort involved in an attack, I'll continue my discussion of password cracking. First, though, one final explanation.

As its name suggests, Hashcat deals with password hashes. Creating a hash in cryptography involves the conversion of a string of characters, such as a password, into a set number of characters, resulting in something a little like a fingerprint. There's no way of undoing or reversing a hash (well, more accurately, it's just really, really difficult to do in reality).

Here are two MD5 examples. First, the hash for the word "hello" is

```
5d41402abc4b2a76b9719d911017c592
```

Second, the MD5 hash for a capitalized "Hello" is

```
8b1a9953c4611296a827abf8c47804d7
```

As you can see, that single uppercase character change makes quite a difference.

Now, if you use another word, "Hello There," you get

```
32b170d923b654360f351267bf440045
```

The MD5 hash of two words is the same length as the previous examples that contained one word. By knowing that your hashes are always the same length, you can tell if a string of seemingly unrelated characters conforms to a standard.

Also, think for a second about why you don't encrypt passwords on a Linux server and then decrypt the system's password file when a user logs in. The answer is simply because the process of encrypting data can be reversed, whereas a one-way function is better than encrypting a password. Some people are surprised to read that the /etc/shadow file doesn't actually remember a user's password at all, just a salted-hash version of it.

Why does an entry in your /etc/shadow password file on Linux look like this? It looks like encryption of some sort at a glance.

```
chrisbinnie:$6$TRIYWb5l$ef6Tm54qpV2nYCn6f20b7w/
5nvp8zpsjacFqeTwqx7fCeW3plG2pkKsGgf1CtWzWhHOPWykFGrfPGmCde4HWY/
:12231:3:32:11:32::
```

The user chrisbinnie has a much longer entry because the Shadow Suite is using a salt to further bolster the passwords. After a user has entered a password on a Linux system, by default, a salt will be used.

In Linux's crypt package for example, this is a two-character string that is chosen from characters in a character set. They could be any of these characters from my English character set (a-z, A-Z, 0-9./). Having chosen a salt, the original algorithm used to hash the user password is then "perturbed" in any of 4,096 different ways. The salt is then saved to the encoded password.

Let's think a little more about Linux passwords for a moment. Modern Linux systems enhance your password security with Shadow passwords. Previously, passwords were stored in the file /etc/passwd, which every user on the system could read. Only root can read the /etc/shadow file, however, and this allows other policies to be enforced properly, such as password aging.

The user login process works like this. When someone logs into a machine, the salt from the relevant entry for their user in the /etc/shadow file is read. Next, the password that the user entered is encoded with the salt that has just been read. The results of this process are checked against the password saved in /etc/shadow. If they are the same, then the user is allowed access. Clever and simple.

One common way of attacking a list of passwords is by knowing, in advance, the hashes for a lot of common passwords and combining them with all of the 4,096 available salt values. This is known as a dictionary attack.

It has been said that today, the bare minimum specification of a secure password system should include an up-to-date hashing algorithm, as well as the resulting hash being salted. Popular modern hashing algorithms include SHA256, SHA512, whirlpool, tiger, ripemd, and SHA3. Each has subtly different attributes.

These algorithms shouldn't be confused with encryption algorithms such as 3DES, Triple DES, Crypt, Blowfish, and Rijndael.

# Using Hashcat

The well-designed, accommodating Hashcat is bundled with a large number of example hashes and wordlists to experiment with. Let's look at how you can work with them.

## Hashcat Capabilities

The general approach of password-cracking tools tends to be one of importing a password file that is full of encrypted data and then generating an output file once the input file has been processed. Let's look at some of the options that are available with the Hashcat tool. I will touch upon some of the other tools that are available from within its software suite in a moment.

Hashcat supports many different types of hashing algorithms, such as MD5, SHA1, and NTLM. In fact, if I'm counting correctly, the number exceeds an incredible 90 varieties. Hashcat claims it can break the MD5 versions of popular applications such as WordPress and Cisco-ASA, and also Drupal7 passwords. In addition to its impressive algorithm support, the many different attack modes that are available include brute forcing passwords, dictionary attacks, rule-based attacks, and fingerprint attacks.

## Installation

At the time of writing, the current version of Hashcat is v2.00. To install Hashcat (assuming that you can't find it in your distribution's repositories), you can head to the website and download the latest binaries. The direct link for v2.00 is here: `https://hashcat .net/files/hashcat-2.00.7z`.

The version 2.00 link is visible at the top of the web page at `https://hashcat.net/ hashcat/`. You should check this page to ensure that you are downloading the latest available version.

Once downloaded, it's just a case of extracting the `.7z` file, and making sure you have the correct permissions to write files to the directory to which you have extracted the files. If you get stuck extracting on any Debian derivatives, then you can install the `7za` package with the following command:

```
# apt-get install p7zip-full
```

9

On Red Hat derivatives, you may need to add a repository. Having done so, the following command will hopefully work for you:

```
# yum install p7zip p7zip-plugins
```

Next, to extract the compressed files and preserve the directory names with x, run the 7za file as follows:

```
# 7za x hashcat-2.00.7z
```

Note the lack of a minus sign before the x, which is the usual convention. That's not a typo.

Having done that, you can now cd into the newly created hashcat-2.00/ directory, which contains many files and subdirectories. Of particular interest are the docs and examples directories, which you can explore to your heart's content. Fear not, you'll look at how to run the Hashcat executable in a moment.

Incidentally, if you're interested in the latest development version, there's a GitHub page at https://github.com/hashcat/hashcat. It also includes documentation and links to the wiki, which should be of interest.

If you're running the sophisticated penetration-testing suite, Kali Linux, then you should be able to install Hashcat as follows, thanks to the fact that it's built-in:

```
# apt-get install hashcat
```

## Hash Identification

There are a couple of things to consider before using Hashcat. You first need to know the type of hash that you are trying to recover the password from.

Let's think about Linux user passwords for a moment. The default hash algorithm in use has changed periodically over time and can also be distribution dependent. In the past, common defaults were MD5 and DES, but SHA512 is now commonplace.

It helps Hashcat if you can identify what hash type you are attacking. You can run the following command to discover which hashing algorithm is in use:

```
# authconfig --test | grep hash
```

If you are concerned about the security on your machine and want to upgrade the hashing algorithm used by your machine's Shadow passwords, then you can use the following command:

```
# authconfig --passalgo=sha512 --update
```

In this example, you can replace sha512 with sha256 if you want. Note, however, that in order to make this change effective, you need to get your users to change their passwords so they are converted to the new hash type. You can expire a user's password, forcing the user to change it at the next login, with the following command:

```
# chage -d 0 chrisbinnie
```

The "change age" command in this example pushes the expiration date to January 1, 1970, which ensures that it's always earlier than the current setting of the system's clock.

Let's look at my example /etc/shadow entry again for the user chrisbinnie:

```
chrisbinnie:$6$TRIYWb5l$ef6Tm54qpV2nYCn6f20b7w/
5nvp8zpsjacFqeTwqx7fCeW3plG2pkKsGgf1CtWzWhHOPWykFGrfPGmCde4HWY/
:12231:3:32:11:32::
```

You don't need to run the authconfig command to determine that the example entry is using a SHA512 hash. You can deduce this by referring to the codes in Table 9.1.

**TABLE 9.1   How to Identify Hashing Algorithms**

| Symbol | Hashing Algorithm |
| --- | --- |
| $0 | DES |
| $1 | MD5 Hashing |
| $2 | Blowfish |
| $2A | Eksblowfish |
| $5 | SHA256 |
| $6 | SHA512 |

In the Shadow password example, sandwiched between two dollar signs directly after the username, there are these three characters: $6$. From Table 9.1 you can tell that the /etc/shadow passwords are using SHA512. This is good news because it's a strong algorithm.

The next section of the password entry, after $6$ and all the way up to the next dollar sign, is the salt. That's TRIYWb5l in this case.

The password (encoded with the salt) is the next section after the dollar sign and up to the first colon. After that, the other sections, within the colons, offer the system some pertinent login information such as when the user's password will expire, when it was last changed, and so on.

To gauge how recently the stronger algorithms have been in use, consider this: according to Fedora, since Fedora 8 the glibc package has supported SHA256 and SHA512 hashes. As a result, from Fedora 9 it has been possible to use SHA256 and SHA512 for passwords.

9

If you're stuck, then check out the website `http://verifier.insidepro.com` to deter-mine which hash variety you want to point Hashcat to. I only had limited success with the example hashes used here, which were generated using a different website's tool, so be warned that it may take you some time to identify an unknown type of hash algorithm.

In case it's useful, try running the following command to generate an MD5 password with a salt (you need `openssl` installed):

```
# openssl passwd -1 -salt 123 PASSWORD
$1$123$YPya29UI1XS9hz1d23ltx/
```

From the results of running that command, note where the $1$ and the 123 are in relation to the encoded password.

I sometimes also run an MD5 hashing test like this (without a salt):

```
# echo PASSWORD | md5sum
8b04b6229e11c290efd5cd8190aa9261   -
```

Other ways of manually generating passwords can be found at `http://unix.stackex-change.com/questions/81240/manually-generate-password-for-etc-shadow`.

## Choosing Attack Mode

Now that you understand how hashes work, let's forge ahead. Even when you know the type of hash that you're dealing with, you still need to consider how to attack any encoded pass-words that you have access to.

I have mentioned a common attack mode referred to as a brute force attack. These attacks will go after the characters that, using U.S. and U.K. character sets at least, will include a-z, A-Z, 0-9./, and so on.

Another popular mode of attack is using wordlists. Here Hashcat will run through pre-defined lists of words, testing if they work with the passwords presented to it.

A more complex way of using wordlists is adding programmed rules, in what Hashcat calls a rule-based attack. You can change and extend words, for example, using custom rules. By crafting some of the finer points of how Hashcat works, your attacks can be more accurate and ultimately more efficient.

## Downloading a Wordlist

If you wanted to run a wordlist attack, you would first need a list of words to check against. There are a few sites online that claim to host lists of leaked passwords.

The site that follows is apparently not involved in nefarious practices. It offers a number of wordlists that you can download. Using an English dictionary as an example, the site will let you download 319,378 words into a list that Hashcat will happily run through. You can find the wordlists at `www.md5this.com/tools/wordlists.html`. (The password to unlock the Zip files containing the words is shown as md5this.com.)

If you're interested, the md5this website also offers a wordlist generator in the form of a python script, which can be downloaded from `www.md5this.com/tools/wordlist-generator.html`. The script works by generating words from website content. In order to run the script, you simply need to point it at a website from where it will scrape its data.

## Rainbow Tables

Instead of leaning on a system's CPU or GPU capacity, another approach is to lean on its storage, potentially using hundreds or thousands of gigabytes. During a brute force attack, rather than calculating a hash on every attempt, it is possible to look up a list of pre-calculated answers held in a long list. These are known as rainbow tables.

There are ways of defeating this approach, namely by using large salts on one-way hashes. This is effective because each password is hashed with a unique salt, and therefore every possible salt's calculated hash would need an entry in a rainbow table alongside its salt.

# Running Hashcat

Now that you know about hashes, attack modes, and where to download a wordlist from (and once you've run through the large number of informative examples, this knowledge can be very useful), you can finally get to running Hashcat itself.

The contents of my installation directory are as follows:

```
charsets/  hashcat-cli32.exe  hashcat-cliXOP.bin  tables/  hashcat-
cli64.app  hashcat-cliXOP.exe
docs/  hashcat-cli64.bin  rules/  hashcat-cli32.bin  examples/
hashcat-cli64.exe  salts/
```

You can see from my directory listing that there are a number of different types of executables.

For your purposes, anything ending in `.bin` will suffice. If for some reason your `.bin` files aren't immediately executable, then as usual you can just type **chmod +x <executable>** to remedy this. I'll be using the 64-bit command line interface version called `hashcat-cli64.bin`, which matches my machine's capabilities.

Apparently, the different Hashcat executables shown in that directory suit a variety of features that might be made available by your machine's processors. The other relevant `.bin` file that you're interested in, with XOP added to its name, stands for eXtended OPerations instructions. If you want to get more serious about using Hashcat later on, you can read up

9

on your processor flags and choose which executable can make best use of your particular system. For example, according to the forums, AMD processor chips suit the XOP version.

Let's now look at running your Hashcat executable. The syntax for the `hashcat` command is as follows:

```
# hashcat [options] hashfile [mask|wordfiles|directories]
```

Having downloaded (or generated) your wordlist and saved it under the filename `wordlist.txt`, you can proceed. Consider this example command after you enter the examples subdirectory with the command `cd examples/`:

```
# ./hashcat-cli64.bin -m0 -a0 A0.M0.hash A0.M0.word
```

The `-m` option means that you are specifying an MD5 hash and the `-a 0` option means you want Hashcat to perform a dictionary attack (also known as a straight attack). For reference, if you had specified `-m1800`, you would be referring to your preferred modern Unix hashing algorithm, SHA512.

As you can probably guess, the `A0.M0.hash` file in the `examples` directory is your list of hashes. These are stripped down without either the `<username>:` section prepending the salt, or the appended password aging information including the colons after it. This is how you should collect hashes.

The `A0.M0.word` file is your potential passwords dictionary as a wordlist.

Incidentally, you could simply add `-o <filename>` if you wanted to output your findings straight to file rather than the screen, or add `--remove` if you wanted to remove a line from your file full of hashes when you had discovered its password.

The results from running the `hashcat` command are as follows (in a heavily abbreviated form):

```
651e96f9b94e1a3a117eade5e226bd1e:y[N"%e?U{<k['x<TlG U6Z
465133fae5a994afb03c7158260b2e8d:kCQArZz)It

All hashes have been recovered
Input.Mode: Dict (A0.M0.word)
Index.....: 1/1 (segment), 102 (words), 2769 (bytes)
Recovered.: 102/102 hashes, 1/1 salts
Speed/sec.: - plains, 102 words
Progress..: 102/102 (100.00%)
Running...: 00:00:00:01
Estimated.: --:--:--:--
```

The first two lines contain the hashes up to the colon, followed by the discovered passwords after the colon. The rest of the output shows you had success across your whole file.

Once you've mastered the examples, try this on your own /etc/shadow hashes. If you're lucky, then after running your adjusted commands, you should be presented with one or more hashes followed by their corresponding passwords in plain text. If you're not getting enough hits, then experiment until you are satisfied with the results. It may take some trial and error to get things working as expected; I would recommend getting comfortable with the comprehensive examples first. If you struggle, then take some comfort from the fact that not all passwords can be broken in an instant.

That said, once you understand the theory and tried using its basic functionality, Hashcat is very simple to operate. From a Linux sysadmin's perspective, this should concern you and you should therefore pay attention to the hashing algorithm that your servers use.

There are a number of options that I will leave you to explore. For example, the option for running rules alongside the sample command is simply -r rules/specific_rule.rule.

I promised that you'd look at some of the corresponding hash values and attack modes. The number of hashes is simply too great to list, but the Hashcat website provides them, along with helpful details, at http://hashcat.net/wiki/doku.php?id=example_hashes.

Some of the attack modes that you can use, with 0 being known as "straight" (in other words, matching against a dictionary or wordlist), are shown in Table 9.2 along with their corresponding numbers.

**TABLE 9.2  Hashcat Attack Modes and Their Corresponding Numbers**

| Number | Attack Mode Description |
| --- | --- |
| 0 | Straight (dictionary and wordlists) |
| 1 | Combination |
| 3 | Brute force (run as part of a mask attack) |
| 6 | Hybrid |

Let's briefly look at the differences between a brute force attack and the dictionary attack you looked at previously.

The main difference between the two relates to brute force attacks having to search through the entire keyspace for a password match. Dictionary attacks, however, only have a limited remit. As a result, dictionary attacks are much quicker, but, of course, there's a good chance they won't crack the salted hashes put in front of them. However, at least you are quickly made aware of any failures with this mode.

This is the opposite of a brute force attack, which will keep running (potentially for a very, very long time) until it succeeds in breaking the password. You are all but assured, if the

9

configuration settings are correct, that you will be handed the password at some point, even if it takes a hundred years for it to happen.

Within its detailed online documentation, Hashcat talks about brute force attacks being an older, less sophisticated route to discovering passwords. Hashcat now includes the brute force style of attack (you may have noticed it mentioned in Table 9.2) within its mask attack mode.

The main premise with a mask attack is to reduce the size of the keyspace and therefore speed up the run time. One clever example that the documentation offers is that with Hashcat's innovative technique, you can reduce the recovery time of the password "Julia1984" from approximately four years to a staggering forty minutes.

The documentation boldly states that there are no disadvantages to running a mask attack over a brute force attack, which is promising. You run a mask attack by appending a mask to the end of your standard command, as follows:

```
# hashcat -m 1800 -a 0 -o discovered_passwords.txt --remove hashes.
txt wordlist.txt -1 ?dabcdef
```

The appended -1 ?dabcdef in this case asks Hashcat to run through the characters 0123456789abcdef.

According to the documentation, this mask, -1 ?l?d?s?u, offers a full 7-bit ASCII character set, also known as mixalpha-numeric-all-space. There are a number of built-in character set options with Hashcat, such as ?l (which stands for all lowercase characters from a to z), and ?u (which stands for all uppercase characters from A to Z).

You can find more details on mask attacks at https://hashcat.net/wiki/doku. php?id=mask_attack.

# oclHashcat

Using oclHashcat and Hashcat requires very similar levels of knowledge, as they operate in almost the same way. Although they have some differences — for example, the way that oclHashcat loads up its dictionaries when compared to Hashcat — you can expect a shallow learning curve if you move over to using oclHashcat.

In addition, the necessary password-cracking computations use an entirely different component of your system, as I have already mentioned. Simply put, oclHashcat works with video cards as opposed to CPUs. There are two important software versions to distinguish between, and each suits two popular GPUs:

- cudaHashcat, which is for use on Nvidia video cards
- oclHashcat, which works with AMD video cards

GPUs are much faster than CPUs (when set up correctly) because they are solely designed to crunch numbers quickly, usually to process graphics. While obviously designed for speed themselves, in terms of performance, CPUs can get distracted with their additional, inclusive feature sets, causing a reduction in throughput. As a result, GPUs are a good choice for computing large amounts of data because they can be optimized much better. It's also possible to scale GPU output almost seamlessly by connecting them together in a chain, making it easier to harness their combined power. To give you an idea of how fast GPUs can be, if you were using rainbow tables and divided the keyspace (of the 95 characters available on a US keyboard), you might hit 10 trillion plain-text tests per second!

In terms of learning Hashcat and oclHashcat, I would recommend getting Hashcat working first and then reading up on how to get your video card's GPU drivers working. There's more information at http://hashcat.net/oclhashcat/.

If it causes confusion, oclHashcat-plus is no longer in use and is considered deprecated. As a result, there's no benefit in the "plus" version.

## Hashcat-Utils

One additional component of the Hashcat suite that is also worth mentioning is a group of utilities called Hashcat-utils. This collection of useful tools can be downloaded from http://hashcat.net/wiki/doku.php?id=hashcat_utils.

The tools include combinator, which is a standalone program from which you can run combinator attacks. You can find more information at https://hashcat.net/wiki/doku.php?id=combinator_attack.

You can also trim and cut up a wordlist file with the cutb tool, which you can use to clean up common, unwanted prepended or appended characters in a wordlist file.

Another tool in the bundle, rli, is similar to the Unix-type command, and simply removes duplicate files, after comparing a file to one or more other files.

It's definitely worth exploring these utilities further to increase your knowledge of how Hashcat works.

## Summary

In this chapter, you looked at some of the theory behind password attacks. I also covered the importance of the number of combinations that a character set includes, the length of passwords, and how their combination affects keyspace. Finally, I described hashing and salting, which ensure that the time it takes to crack a password is significantly increased.

Being able to efficiently crack a password takes years to master, and it's certainly an area with many facets. However, the venerable Hashcat helps you to make light work of the learning process. It also has a detailed FAQ that can be found at `http://hashcat.net/wiki/doku.php?id=frequently_asked_questions`.

Having now seen the methods that an attacker will use to crack your passwords, and the ways that you can make their work more difficult, you should pay close attention if you discover traces of any of the tools that I've discussed on your own machines. With your new-found power, there's hopefully no need to remind you to use your skills responsibly.

# SQL Injection Attacks

One of the most popular types of online attacks is known as SQL injection, sometimes abbreviated as SQLi. These attacks involve the insertion of database code using Structured Query Language (SQL), where attackers can retrieve data from databases or overwrite existing data.

You might be surprised to learn that, according to OWASP (the Open Web Application Security Project), which is a charitable organization that promotes the securing of software, SQLi was the number one threat to online services in 2013, and listed as the most common threat at https://www.owasp.org/index.php/Top_10_2013-Top_10.

This chapter looks at what these attacks involve, how to protect your websites against them, and finally how to launch them yourself for the purposes of penetration testing.

Needless to say, this is a wide and complex area that requires a degree of background knowledge to carry out more sophisticated attacks. You might be surprised how easy it is, however, having run only a handful of commands and with only a little database knowledge, to bring a vulnerable online service to its knees. For that reason alone, it's imperative that IT professionals be aware of the risks that SQL injections pose and how to mitigate their effects.

## History

Considering its simplicity, the fact that SQLi is so effective makes it a formidable type of attack.

Take note, junior developers, because when it comes to security matters, sysadmins tend not to be directly responsible for such attacks occurring. This is because much of the time, the exploits are possible due to code that does not escape special characters properly. In addition to its simplicity, another cause for concern is that this type of attack has reportedly been known about since 1998. An issue of *Phrack Magazine*, published in December of that year, first announced a broad, sweeping vulnerability against websites. The horror began to unfold over time, and it became obvious that several automated tools could be used to sweep the web, looking for sites, and then deface or steal data from them as they saw fit.

It didn't stop there, however. As phishing attacks became more popular (where attackers trick users into revealing information about themselves), cunning attackers went about completely rebranding a website, by injecting the necessary code to persuade a visitor that they were visiting a bona fide website.

For a number of years, I ran a very small co-location server ISP for relatively tech-savvy customers. On at least three occasions, our co-located server customers, who had unwittingly been less diligent with their server-side scripting, succumbed to phishing attacks. From the mid-2000s onwards, over the space of just a few years, the U.S. Federal Bureau of Investigation was in touch with us, a bank on one occasion, and a white hat security service on another, informing us that a customer server had been hacked. So, even in such a small organization, a bogus copy of a popular auction site and two banking websites had been cloned and used in phishing attacks on our networks within a very short space of time. It quickly became obvious that SQLi attacks were becoming popular among those with nefarious intent.

In reaction to the common security threat, sysadmins and developers took note and began hardening code. I remember diligently escaping special characters with every user input component on a PHP-based website around that time to avoid SQLi attacks.

# Basic SQLi

As I have already alluded to, the main premise behind SQLi is illegitimately retrieving code from or injecting code into a database.

To avoid these issues, you can no longer expose queries to the outside via server-side languages, which will make your websites far less fluid and less useful as a result. Failing that, you can make sure that all attack vectors are covered. The easiest way to achieve this is to filter all input that you receive from visitors. In other words, at every point on your website where a user can input data, you need to take relevant precautions within your code. This involves parsing the input into a friendly format before that data is sent to your database.

A full tutorial on how you might go about securing your code can be left for another day. However, I will give you a quick refresher using one popular programming language. Before that, I'll remind you of some simple ways that SQLi works.

As I've said, simply defacing a website is far from the only damage that intercepted SQL can cause. Consider this SQL statement, for example:

```
sql-server> DROP TABLE special-offers;
```

By knowing table names, you can completely delete a table from a database. Aside from destructive behavior, I haven't mentioned the extraction of usernames and passwords from a database. With criminal intent, a successful SQL attack is without question a prize worth pursuing. Some sizeable brands have fallen victim to poorly programmed code and SQLi. Reportedly, Yahoo, Adobe, LinkedIn, and Sony Music might all be included on a long list of victims. Of course, without being one of the attackers, or the staff who had to recover services affected by such attacks, I can only conjecture to what extent these attacks involved SQLi. A SQLi Hall of Shame can be found at http://codecurmudgeon.com/wp/sql-injection-hall-of-shame/. Although the list may not be completely accurate, I am sure you will agree that it is a compelling read.

A moment ago, I referred to a programming language. I'll use what is reportedly the world's most popular server-side scripting language, PHP, as an example to quickly demonstrate how SQLi works. As well as being used directly on millions of websites, the powerful PHP is used in the world's most popular Content Management System (CMS), WordPress (https://wordpress.com), and many other dynamic website applications such as Joomla! (https://www.joomla.org). In short, PHP is all over the web and is an easy target for attackers if an exploit is discovered.

Let's look at another example, but this time in PHP:

```
$input = $variable[3];
$dbquery = "SELECT id, item, price FROM specialoffers ORDER BY id
LIMIT 15 OFFSET $input;";
```

Looking at the top line, you can see that you are not filtering the variable called $input. This means that when the variable is used on the second line within the SQL statement, it could potentially include any code that an attacker wanted to use. With crafted code being injected, all sorts of havoc can be caused.

Another example would be updating the sysop user's password. For example, a normal SQL statement inside PHP code might look like this:

```
$dbquery = "UPDATE credentials SET passwd='$password' WHERE
userid='$id';";
```

By appending SQL to this statement, such as or userid like '%sysop%', your SQL becomes much less strict and you ask the database to quickly search for other privileged usernames similar to sysop, such as sysops, and then update their passwords too.

Worryingly, it's also possible to execute shell commands that can be included within SQL. Certain database servers allow access to operating system commands using this method.

# Mitigating SQLi in PHP

As I've said, this subject area is too large to cover in detail, but I would be remiss not to briefly look at how to filter SQL inputs to help mitigate SQLi attacks. There are a variety of PHP functions that assist you in this endeavor. As of this writing, PHP is making a significant move to version 7.0.0 from its current version, 5.6.16 (although it will likely be incremented).

One caveat would be that in older versions (up to 5.3.0), inside your main PHP config file (php.ini) it was possible to filter (or escape) all input data via PHP by using magic_quotes_gpc. This was apparently deprecated because it was relied upon too much and didn't always escape characters in the way that meant applications were secured. In essence, magic quotes weren't designed to be used for security purposes but were employed as such.

10

To protect the variable used in the first SQL example, you might want to run your user input through the `stripslashes` function. The example looked like this:

```
$input = $variable[3];
```

With stripslashes being used, it might look something like this:

```
$input = stripslashes($variable[3]);
```

As you would guess, this means you are removing slashes to help protect against unwelcome input. There's also `trim` for removing white space from a variable, which can be used in the same way, as well as `strip_tags` for removing HTML and other markup tags. These can all be useful and possibly chained together for ease, like this:

```
$input = stripslashes((trim($input));
```

In addition, up to PHP version 5.5.0, you could use the `mysql_real_escape_string` function to clean up individual strings as follows:

```
$input = mysql_real_escape_string($input);
```

However, as of version 7.0.0 and up, you almost always want to use an improved driver called `MySQLi` (which stands for MySQL improved) to counter SQLi. Thanks to this enhancement, you can employ a more advanced way to strip unnecessary and potentially dangerous characters out of the code being executed. An example using `mysqli` doesn't look all that different from the previous example:

```
$input= mysqli_real_escape_string($input);
```

Using MySQLi, you connect to your database using a different method, as follows:

```
$mysqli = new mysqli("localhost", "userid", "passwd", "DB_name");
```

Another approach to mitigating SQLi attacks is when you use prepared statements. The idea behind this security addition is for the database engine to process SQL completely separately from any parameters being used. In theory, this means an attacker cannot inject code into the query at all. An example might look like this:

```
$input = $mysqli->prepare("INSERT INTO table_name (column_name)
VALUES (?)");
$input->bind_param("s", $actual_user_input);
$input->execute();
$input->close();
```

This newer, preferred approach filters out your parameters using the new library. Note the question mark where the variable's value would usually have gone previously. The line containing `execute` pulls together all of the previous parameters. Of additional help is that such a function only needs to be read once, so if it's run a number of times on a few pages, then the PHP engine does less work.

Another approach to be aware of has been available since earlier versions of PHP and makes use of PHP Data Objects (PDO). There's a helpful lengthy discussion here: http://stack-overflow.com/questions/60174/how-can-i-prevent-sql-injection-in-php.

It's debatable as to which methodology is the best to use, but PDO seems very popular. An example of PDO would look like this:

```
$input = $pdo->prepare('SELECT * FROM special_offers_table WHERE
offer = :specialoffer');
$input->execute(array('name' => $specialoffer));
```

There's some well-written information about PDO at http://whateverthing.com/blog/2014/08/28/the-heart-of-darkness/. It's worth reading, if for no other reason than to help you choose between methods in the later versions of PHP (version 7.0.0 and onwards) to combat SQLi threats.

# Exploiting SQL Flaws

Now that you've looked at a few different ways to secure against SQLi, you will learn how a hacker might attack your online service. Although there are a number of tools available, I'll focus on sqlmap (http://sqlmap.org), which is a popular, open-source tool among hackers, forensic scientists, and penetration testers. It's possible to wreak chaos with this highly sophisticated tool, so make sure that you are fully aware of the damage you can do when testing it on your own servers, never mind servers that belong to others. I would definitely recommend using a development server or sandbox virtual machine to be safe.

The widespread compatibility of sqlmap is enough to give most diligent sysadmins cause for concern. According to its website, sqlmap supports the following database servers: MySQL, Oracle, PostgreSQL, Microsoft SQL Server, Microsoft Access, IBM DB2, SQLite, Firebird, Sybase, SAP MaxDB, and HSQLDB.

Let's look at how you install sqlmap. It's bundled with some security-based distributions such as Kali Linux, but if it's not in your package manager's repositories, then there are alternative ways to install it.

You can use GitHub's sqlmap repository by using the Git clone command:

```
# git clone https://github.com/sqlmapproject/sqlmap.git sqlmap-dev
```

There's also a Zip file available from https://github.com/sqlmapproject/sqlmap/zipball/master.

You can also download a tarball from `https://github.com/sqlmapproject/sqlmap/tarball/master`.

Once you have followed the installation instructions, you should be able to get to the stage where the following command will work (after running the previous Git command, this is all you need to do to get started):

```
# cd sqlmap-dev
# python ./sqlmap.py -h
```

This command will offer you a list of options.

# Launching an Attack

Let's now look at the core of sqlmap's functionality, namely compromising a remote machine.

Be warned, however, that a time-consuming aspect of testing your sqlmap skills will likely either involve setting up your own test server to be vulnerable, or legitimately identifying websites that are vulnerable to attack. You might be surprised to read that, because of the way URLs are formed, Google can identify vulnerable sites very easily. It hopefully goes without saying that I do not advocate attacking any of the sites that you find using Google or through any other method, for that matter. For the purposes of spotting potentially exploitable URLs, however, you can enter a query such as `inurl:website.php?id=` or `inurl:product.php?id=`. The first search term returns a very worrying 1.7 million results.

Websites and other online resources that incompetently expose their vulnerabilities via Google have earned a nickname, Googledorks. There's a site that lists some of them; it's worth a quick look and can be found at `www.hackersforcharity.org/ghdb/`. The lists include a number of potentially secret login pages, sensitive directories, and files that mention usernames. Use this information responsibly.

Incidentally, you can run sqlmap via Python, which means you will need an implementation of one type or another installed on your machine.

In Figure 10.1 you can see that the developers are keen to distance themselves from illegal activity. Such powerful tools are always subject to abuse.

Let's continue on. Looking at the following example, the syntax that is required to use the `sqlmap` command is quite simple:

```
# python sqlmap.py -u "http://www.a-vulnerable-website.com/product
.php?id=1111"
```

**FIGURE 10.1**

How sqlmap looks when you launch it, disclaimer included

If you are either using slow connectivity or experiencing slow responses from the remote database server, then you can append `--time-sec 10` to that command to introduce a more realistic time-out setting. Somewhat counterintuitively, this can actually speed up the overall process.

Now let's methodically step through a few simple commands. You may choose to chain these all together once you become familiar with using sqlmap.

My sqlmap example command includes the `-u` option, which means that a URL is declared. That command will simply check for vulnerabilities for the trailing parameter (`id=1111`) using a number of SQL injection tests. From there, sqlmap can normally detect the web server vendor and version, the remote operating system, and the version of the database server that is in use.

What if you now want to learn the names of the databases in use by the website in question? You can do this by adding the `--dbs` option as follows:

```
# python sqlmap.py -u "http://www.a-vulnerable-website.com/product
.php?id=1111" --dbs
```

Having retrieved that useful information, your next step would be to discover the table names that are in use. You can do that as follows, substituting your real database name with the `<database-name>` entry:

```
# python sqlmap.py -u "http://www.a-vulnerable-website.com/product
.php?id=1111" --tables -D <database-name>
```

The next logical step would be to learn the columns used by a database table of interest. The command is simply as follows, again substituting your database name with the `<database-name>` entry, and also `<table-name>` with your table name:

```
# python sqlmap.py -u "http://www.a-vulnerable-website.com/product
.php?id=1111" --columns -D <database-name> -T <table-name>
```

10

The final part of the process would be pulling all of the data from your target database. This might include usernames and passwords, personal customer information, or simply product information for an online shop. If you are attacking a remote site, how valuable the information you extract is clearly depends on the site you are interfacing with. To dump the database data, you introduce the --dump option as shown here:

```
# python sqlmap.py -u "http://www.a-vulnerable-website.com/product.
php?id=1111" --dump --columns -D <database-name> -T <table-name>
```

If you want to only pull down specific columns, then you can specify them directly. Once you know the column names, you can simply list them with an option such as -C columnX, columnY and separate them with commas. Having done so, you just remove the --columns option included in the previous example.

Your last command might produce output something like this:

```
+--------+----------------+----------+----------+-------------+--------------+
| id     | title          | color    | price    | category    | received-date|
+--------+----------------+----------+----------+-------------+--------------+
| 1111   | bars of soap   | green    | 1.22     | toiletries  | 11.11.22     |
+--------+----------------+----------+----------+-------------+--------------+
```

If you are a developer or sysadmin and you're not concerned with how quickly a database dump occurs, then you certainly should be. Keep in mind that you could have used Google to identify a list of potential targets with minimal effort and through only a handful of commands gotten to the stage of stealing potentially valuable commercial data. In addition to this data theft, you can also overwrite the existing data and deface the online service in question using sqlmap, to the detriment of their brand and reputation, with relative ease.

The powerful and sophisticated sqlmap tool provides you with a lengthy list of options that are simply too great to cover in detail. I would suggest reading the GitHub page, which gives you more details about using sqlmap. It can be found at https://github.com/sqlmapproject/sqlmap/wiki/Usage.

# Trying SQLi Legally

There are likely a number of useful websites that allow you to run scans in order to confirm that you have configured your penetration-testing tools correctly. One such site that you may want to test your new-found SQLi skills on is called Web Scan Test. A SQL injection is possible via this subdirectory: www.webscantest.com/datastore. However, I would read the site's terms before proceeding, just to be sure you're not committing a crime.

An online demo might also be of interest from the Codebashing website. They describe their clever, interactive website as "[a]pplication security training for programmers, by programmers." The demo runs through how special characters make a massive difference to a login process, and it walks you through how the underlying database server reacts as you change your input. You can find the demo at www.codebashing.com/sql_demo.

# Summary

In this chapter, I have covered the basics behind SQL injection and also briefly looked at the history of SQL attacks. In addition, you saw how PHP developers have recommended protecting against MySQL-related SQLi attacks, both in the past for older versions and moving forward for newer versions, after version 7.0.0 in particular.

It's easy to see why SQLi attacks are so common — and in fact have been considered the most popular type of attack in some arenas. Using a few relatively simple sqlmap commands, you wielded the power to potentially breach a website's security, and then query and steal its valuable data, only to then go on to further damage its reputation with vandalism.

It's important for technical personnel defending against such attacks to be aware of how simple these attacks are, and to understand the implications of apparently simple mistakes. Those mistakes can open up websites — which likely took a lot of effort and resources to build — to devastating attacks that cost a great deal to recover from. Once again, use these skills responsibly. It's much more satisfying to protect your own infrastructure properly than to attack infrastructure that belongs to others.

10

# Index